PARENTING
EMOTIONALLY
DISTRESSED
KIDS

Copyright © 2023 by Dr. Michelle Alden
All rights reserved.

No part of this book may be reproduced or transmitted in any form or by any means, electronic or mechanical, including photocopying, recording, or by any information storage and retrieval system, without written permission from the publisher. For all inquiries please contact Innovator Press at www.InnovatorPress.com.

ISBN (paperback) 979-8-9851902-7-4
ISBN (ebook) 979-8-9851902-6-7

Lead Editor: Kevin Mullani
Editor: Tess Bohls

Cover & Interior Design: Innovator Press
www.InnovatorPress.com

Printed in the United States

ADVANCE PRAISE

"Michelle's work with families and individuals is life changing for so many! She has wisdom in the dynamics of family life, and assist families in applying therapeutic interventions. She is gifted and a true credit to the counseling profession."

—**Kristin Staley**
LCPC, MA, MBA

"Our family had lost track of what it was like to be a family. We were fighting one battle after the next and never having time to breathe. After Healthy Foundations we started to enjoy each other again and finally became the family we had hoped to be. The chaos, fear, and stress was replaced with respect, goals, games and time together."

—**Jamie W.**

"This program has helped create a foundational modality for our agency to treat families in our community."

—**Dallen Bell, LPC**

"The support and structure of the program as well as the adaptations to fit the specific circumstances of the family really helped work toward a new baseline and further build the relationships of our family."

—**Matt Willett**

"After adopting through foster care our home wasn't safe and even the doctors and specialists we talked to couldn't tell us how to get safety back in our home. Michelle's program worked and it still feels miraculous years later. We are all forever changed and I am incredibly grateful."

—**Jo Wenger**

"The HF Family Program was life altering. I highly recommend putting the work in now. I was looking for residential for an 8 year old and feeling like a failure. Now I have a home I want to live in with people I am glad to spend time with."

—**Tamara Joslin**

"Having worked in the pediatric occupational therapy field for the last twelve plus years I have, at times, felt limited as to how much assistance I can actually provide for parents with behaviorally challenging kiddos. During my internship with Michelle, I was delighted to learn that there was in-home help available to parents. Our clinic confidentially refers families to the Healthy Foundations Family Program so that parents can regain hope in their ability to learn and apply the skills needed to be the best they can for their children."

—**Donna Urrabazo**
COTA/L, Idaho Therapy Source

"You can't love the trauma out of someone, but by building safety and connection your kiddos will feel safe and your home will no longer be a war zone. Michelle's unique approach to parenting hard kiddos was effective and it works! I was definitely skeptical at first but following her direction and putting in the hard work definitely paid off! If we expect our kiddos to work hard and do better, we as parents must put in the same hard work!""

—**Tiffany Buch**

PARENTING EMOTIONALLY DISTRESSED KIDS

Build a Bridge to Better Behavior
the Healthy Foundations Way

DR. MICHELLE ALDEN

INNOVATOR
PRESS

Boise, Idaho

CONTENTS

FOREWORD VII
INTRODUCTION 1
CHAPTER 1 9
   How Did We Get Here?
CHAPTER 2 19
   What's Going on in Your Child's Brain?
CHAPTER 3 31
   Highly Frustrated and Inflexible
CHAPTER 4 47
   Safety
CHAPTER 5 59
   Regulation
CHAPTER 6 71
   Structure
CHAPTER 7 81
   Connection
CHAPTER 8 93
   The Value of Relationships
CHAPTER 9 105
   Setting Goals and Building Motivation
CHAPTER 10 117
   Tips and Tools to Build a Better Bridge
CHAPTER 11 125
   Bridge to Change and Future
ACKNOWLEDGEMENTS 135

FOREWORD

I must start by stating that raising a healthy child is the most difficult task there is. I found myself thinking and saying this statement for decades before I got my big chance to find out if it is true. One day, in front of me were two parents seeking my help with a challenging child. One was a professor at a university who taught neuroscience and the other was a real-life rocket scientist. You likely have heard the expression, *well it's not rocket science*. Here was my chance to see which was more difficult—rocket science or parenting. If you guessed I was told it was the latter, you are correct. The aerospace engineer was quick to say, "Math, physics and aerodynamics all have constants and are predictable, unlike a child!" So there it was—parenting, particularly with a challenging child (aren't they all to some degree), is the world's most difficult task even more so than rocket science!

Scientists must work for decades to learn their trade. However, it is unlikely that parents reading this book have a doctorate in parenting (does that even exist?), or perhaps even have attended a few parenting classes before their bundle of joy arrived in the family. To put this situation in perspective, we have the world's most difficult assignment (parenting) with the most important of outcomes on society (the resulting adult) and are provided little to no training or experience. If you have read books and perhaps even taken parenting classes then you are among the most informed of parents, and likely even then you find your knowledge and skills less than adequate. Regardless of your preparation to becoming a parent, you likely have significant 'on the job training,' for better or worse. Wherever you fit in these categories, you have found a book that will provide you new insights as well as additional tools to help send your child toward becoming a healthy adult.

Excuse me for neglecting to introduce myself. I always want to know a writer or presenter's background to help me determine the potential wisdom of their ideas. I am a psychologist and family therapist with a 52-year professional career. Despite having the opportunity to reach the highest levels of graduate education, my career and my deeper understanding really began when emotionally disturbed children became my instructors. After ten years as an outpatient professional therapist, I changed course in order to reach the most disturbed and challenging children in our society, and I quite literally brought my most difficult young clients into my home. Living for decades in the same home with the most violent and aggressive young children we could find may leave you feeling sorry for my dear wife (of 51 years). But in my defense, we had a written prenuptial agreement that warned her of what to expect. However the reality surprised both of us. Our home became a healing center for thousands of angry, battered and oppositional children over the decades.

I hope it is clear that with a combination of my psychological education and training, but more so my direct first-hand experience, I know some things about parenting the difficult child. Having said that, I encourage you to prepare yourself to receive in this book many keys to success that few parents are afforded. I can tell you that the principles you are about to read actually work, and the degree to which they will help you will in large part depend on your investment and sweat equity you put into your parenting.

For years I was challenged continually to write down what I was learning from my young instructors about effective parenting and finally agreed to do so. Over twenty years this turned into ten books on how to understand the most challenging children and help them become functional adults and contributing members of society. You will find many aspects of what

I learned in the following pages. For example:

- The important balance of authoritarian vs. permissive, or 'soft parenting.'
- Effective and successful parenting requires that the adult is in charge even if control is granted to the child at times. The only way a child can be safe and healthy is in the presence of competent adult.
- Parents can be the most important therapeutic agents in a child's life.
- You can't come up with a successful solution to problem behavior unless you focus on the right problem and not simply focus on the symptom(s).
- Until a child's brain functions adequately (executive functions), the adult's brain must fill the gap.
- Understanding the child's brain and making a positive impact on how it functions is a key to success.

This is only the beginning of what you will learn in these pages. Without specifically discussing the basic needs of children, this book integrates important needs into each chapter. We all know a child needs safety, food, clothing, shelter and clean air and water. But struggling children have a much longer list of basic needs that include: love, stability and predictability, touch, learning and education, healing the past, personal expression, physical and mental health as well as higher order needs of joy, hope, self-determination and happiness (yes we are back to the world's most difficult job). Only when these needs are met can we expect a young person to become a successful adult and meet these needs in future generations, otherwise the cycle of human failure is repeated.

Parenting may be the most difficult job, but in so many ways a good parent is and always has been the answer to the question of what is most important for a child growing up. Perhaps you give yourself credit for all the effort you have put into your child, if so, good for you! But if you are like the majority of parents who struggle with the tribulations of modern parenting, I hope you will take me very seriously when I say a key element for you to maintain your sanity is—no one can ask or expect more of you than your best!

I mentioned earlier that I always note the background of authors and presenters. When encountering trainers, I usually can tell within minutes if the individual has actually *been there*, meaning has parented one or more challenging children. I do not agree that experts must always have experienced the same situation as those they help. I believe I have something to offer someone with cancer or someone struggling with suicidal issues, although I have experienced neither. At the same time with some issues, particularly with parenting, there is no substitute for living it and the depth of wisdom this experience provides. I believe you will agree with me after reading this book that Dr. Alden is also someone who has learned firsthand through her parenting experiences.

As with all learning opportunities, read these pages with an open mind and one that is ready to learn and try something new or adjust what is not entirely new. As Dr. Alden would be the first to say, this book will not provide all the answers you need and is only another stone for the bridge to your success. When it comes to parenting, never stop learning!

Because it is a tremendous source of psychological and spiritual growth, I wish you many challenges in your parenting, and I also wish you great success!

—**Dave Ziegler, Ph.D., L.M.F.T.**
Licensed Psychologist, Family Therapist, and Author,
but most importantly, Foster Parent to hundreds of difficult children

INTRODUCTION

You are exhausted. You feel fed up with raising a struggling child. You believe you've tried everything, but can't seem to make progress. Your home is chaotic, you feel like your family is falling apart, and you sometimes wonder, "Why is my kid acting like this and what am I doing wrong?" You may even be worried about violent or out-of-control behaviors that you fear will cause police or state involvement. No amount of therapy, counseling, or medication seems to affect your child's behavior, and you have concern for their survival, let alone a positive future. Eventually, at your wit's end, you just want someone to "fix" your child.

Don't worry, *you are not alone!*

Even if things have not gotten this bad but you want a little more peace and cooperation in your home, there are things you can do that will help. Even if you have spent years looking for help and trying all kinds of other solutions—play therapy, family therapy, community-based services, medications, and talk therapy—but there are still distressing behaviors, mental health issues, and a growing number of diagnoses … there is still hope!

I totally understand you want some "expert" out there to tell you what is wrong with your child and what to do to fix him or her. Your journey has been a long one, especially if school experts, counselors, neighbors, and maybe even your own family members are acting like it's your fault. This can be especially draining and cause you to question your own sanity. The unfortunate truth, however, is that many of the "experts" are likely as confused and frustrated as you are. They don't know what to do either.

The social systems in place may seem lacking when it comes to helping your child's behaviors and moods. This causes parents to lose trust in them, especially after years of therapy and advice, long wait lists, poorly trained providers who don't really understand what is going on with your child, or how hard things are at home. Couple this with the fact that your child appears to be making good progress while in the counselor's office, but nothing changes at home, and you continue to fear that everything is actually your fault. Please, let me reassure you: it's not!

I applaud you for continuing to try—for searching for the right therapist, treatment, medication, or placement. Ultimately, you know something has to change. At my parent-centered agency in Idaho, we believe parents who have children with emotional and behavioral challenges often struggle to successfully parent their children. Therefore, we offer parent training and guided support *in* the home.

There is a strong belief in our society—and especially within the systems that provide care for children—that a child's behavioral, emotional, and mental health problems can best be dealt with by "experts" outside of the home. At the same time, there is a great deal of blame that goes back and forth between these systems and the parents. Depending on your child's age, you may have already felt separated from the work going on with your child in therapy or at school. You probably feel like they know best. However, I don't believe they know best and I think there is a much more effective approach.

I believe parents need tools and support to be more effective at parenting in general, which helps to establish safety in their homes and move them forward with greater hope and confidence. Parents also need guidance on how to implement these tools and to receive support through the challenges they are facing. But they **don't** need someone else to raise their child because

INTRODUCTION

they are an "expert." I know this is true because I've seen it over and over, with family after family. With the right process, tools, and support, you **can** take back control and have the safe, loving, calm family you long for inside. That is what you will learn from this book. But first, let me tell you why I am so passionate about helping families with challenging children.

MY PERSONAL STORY

I was the middle child, born into a family that was falling apart. My biological mother did not raise her four children—she gave us up for adoption before the oldest was six years old. The years before adoption were pretty dark, and were filled with abuse and neglect. My brothers and I were placed for adoption into foster care when I was five years old. My younger brother was adopted quickly, but my brother Jack and I spent about a year in foster care. Jack was reckless, angry, and loaded with behavioral problems. He was in and out of many homes prior to our adoptive placement, where we were adopted together. My adoptive parents did all they could, along with the social worker and a team of counselors and psych doctors, but Jack was filled with rage. He ran away, was aggressive and out of control, unattached, and needed more than anyone was able to do for him. He was placed in a boys' home for a while until his maternal birth-grandparents adopted him back into the family. Truthfully, I was somewhat relieved that he was gone; he had threatened my well-being many times. However, the way that he left caused me to live with the fear that I would be sent away as well.

I was blessed to have structure, expectations, and support to move away from my early childhood trauma while growing up in my adoptive home. At that time, there was no such thing as schools or parenting methods that were trauma-informed. I struggled with the need to belong, but I worked hard to fit in. I wanted to build relationships and connect, and I had a strong sense of God and faith, even as a child. For some crazy reason, at twelve years old, I started reading all the parenting books my mother had. I knew I wanted a family and I wanted to work with children that were like my brother, Jack, but I had no idea at that time how I could do so. Meanwhile, my parents kept me busy with school, sports, and working on our ranch. I would say I thrived, even though I had a deeper longing for family and belonging. I did well in school and went on to college, where I pursued my dream to work with troubled youth. I was a youth pastor for a time and my love for working with difficult children and seeing them change for the better grew.

As a parent, I raised five biological children and later adopted a twelve-year-old boy from foster care. Early in my childrearing time, I also worked with a camp for abused children who were in foster care. This work changed me as a parent and as a person, allowing me to heal my own childhood wounds from foster care and adoption. I started seeing behaviors as a form of communication and learned the power of connection so I could move in closer to help people with their struggles. I started a non-profit that ran camps and activities for at-risk youth in the community where I lived. Here, I trained volunteers to work with challenging children; this laid the foundation for the program I began in 2013, which was designed to teach parents how to raise challenging children.

Finally, I completed my doctorate in human services and organizational leadership to take my knowledge even further and ensure I was constantly learning in order to help as much as possible. Altogether, I've been helping struggling children and their families for over twenty years with an incredibly high success rate. Unfortunately, not every state has a program like mine to help. Even if they do, the wait list or accessibility may prevent struggling families from getting help. That is why I was moved to write this book. I needed to share my program with as many families as possible, without having to be in the home myself. I do this through a twelve-week process that I relate to a stone arch bridge.

THE BRIDGE AND STONES

Bridges are structures built to span physical obstacles such as ravines, valleys, roads, or rivers. A bridge can also metaphorically connect ideas, hopes, or dreams that are not yet realized by allowing a person to reach a future setting or mindset. You may be hoping for better connection with your children, less stress and chaos, children who listen and do what you tell them, more togetherness, and fun family time. Or, you may be looking for safety in your home, hope for the future, and the confidence you need

INTRODUCTION

as a parent to feel successful through the challenges you face in raising your children. My framework, the *Healthy Foundations Family Program*®, is the bridge that can help you reach your family goals. It is made up of foundational stones that teach you the skills, tools, and tips needed to build a bridge for yourself and your family. Building this bridge is an ongoing process. The program is designed to give you some of the major stones and the tools to put them in place. Once you start to build, you will be able to move into the promising future you all deserve.

One of the first families that used this framework had adopted three children from foster care. The children were ages ten, nine, and four, and all three had been exposed to drugs and alcohol. The oldest and youngest were biologically related and were placed into their adoptive home as babies. The dynamic was challenging, as you can imagine. Despite years of taking parenting courses and getting help from all kinds of experts, the situation continued to spiral downward. Sitting together to enjoy a meal seemed impossible, and it wasn't even safe to ride in the same car to family outings or church. They tried increasing medication and getting more support staff at school, but nothing was helping. They were constantly in crisis or survival mode. Finally, out of desperation, they reached out to me and asked to try the program I had just developed that focused on developing in-home skills and tools.

Using the same framework in this book, the parents were able to see amazing changes in their family. There were challenges and bumps in the road, but the framework provided a bridge from where they were—in crisis, chaos, and daily struggles—to safety in the home, children off of their medication, and being able to enjoy family time. The children were happier and started to enjoy success at school and graduated, able to walk into much more promising futures. A few years after the program, the family took a cross-country road trip together to visit relatives on the east coast. I marveled with them that they were able to travel together for days at a time, all in one vehicle. Was it perfect? No, of course not. But the parents had the tools and structure in place to handle the difficulties that came up. Furthermore, the problems fell in line with normal traveling issues that all families experience with children and long car trips. We all consider it a huge success!

WILL THE FAMILY PROGRAM WORK FOR MY FAMILY?

Bridges are designed differently based on their purpose. Whether you have a footbridge that only needs to support a few people, or you have a highway bridge that needs to support semi-trucks constantly crossing with large loads, they all need to provide a safe way to cross from one place to another. A great deal of a bridge's success depends on the engineer designing the best bridge for the purpose. But the rest is up to the builders to follow the blueprint from the engineer and complete the bridge. I have engineered a bridge to serve the purpose of taking your family across this hard time. It's also important to know that the design of the framework does not need to be altered because of individual family dynamics. I have found that regardless of family diversity, number of children, parenting skills and experience, or socio-economic status, those who are determined and committed to build the bridge successfully cross their difficulties to a healthier functioning family. So yes, the Family Program will work for your family … if you're willing to put in the work and build the bridge.

WHAT TO EXPECT

The goal of this book is to form a bridge made of guiding principles that will take you from where your family is now to the family you wish to have. It follows the outline of the Healthy Foundations Family Program, which became a statewide accepted program in Idaho in 2019. It is unique in that it is designed to help parents learn the tools needed to successfully raise their children, even during challenging times and behaviors.

The coming chapters will explain the stones required for a happier, healthier family and how to put them in place. The way we interact in our homes and the safety we create and uphold is the single most important factor to making changes in the family and in your child. So, this will be the first stone presented. Other stones you will learn how to put in place are structure, regulation, connection, and many more. All of the stones have value and are useful to make positive changes in your family, your role as parents, and your child's behavior. Of course, I'll also highlight how your

INTRODUCTION

family's hopes, values, traditions, and personalities are part of the cement that will hold those stones in place as you build.

Before I get to the stones, I need to provide some background and a little foundational education that is critical to your success. So, if you're ready to finally take back control in your household, help your child develop into their full potential, and have the peace, love, and joy you've been dreaming of within your family, let's get started.

CHAPTER 1

How Did We Get Here?

Did you know that one out of five children in the United States experience a mental health disorder each year? According to the Centers for Disease Control and Prevention, most of these diagnoses are behaviorally based and occur during the first few years of school. There has been a rise in mental health related emergency visits for children ages 5-11 since 2020.[1] The signs indicate that the mental health of our children is deteriorating in our nation. Currently one of the biggest worries for parents is the rise of children's mental health issues.

The families I help typically have children that are angry, defiant, aggressive, and difficult. They will argue all day long about even the most basic things. I work in homes where children have seriously hurt one or both of their parents, siblings, household pets, or other children. While they are also described as sweet and caring, this may only be when they want something. Parents are exhausted and frustrated, tired of dealing with behaviors that make no sense and seem to have no resolution. They feel burned out, hopeless, and are worried about messing up their child for life. This situation is quite alarming for children and adults, so what in the world is happening?

HOW DID WE GET HERE?

Children today are not the same as the children your parents or grandparents raised. Parenting is certainly not the same for many parents today. I have found that children aren't passing through the "terrible twos" any more. Most parents will tell you this stage doesn't go away. Even at five, ten, or fourteen years old, children throw tantrums similar to the ones they should have left behind at two years old. Modern approaches to parenting and mental health are creating children who are strong-willed, unafraid to speak their minds, and basically unconcerned about socially acceptable behaviors. These children try to control everything and everyone around them, or feel entitled to make every choice and decision about their day. I believe this huge change in behavior problems and mental health issues is due in part to central changes in the way we view and raise children. Not every child is severely affected by this change, but what we are doing as a whole is not working for the majority of children, despite moving away from traditional and non-traditional parenting.

Parenting no longer fits into the classic camps of traditional or non-traditional. Most parents I work with don't even know how to define traditional parenting, except to say that it was the way they were raised, or even the way their parents were raised. While their great-grandparents may have been raised in a traditional two-parent home, with a stay-at-home mother and working father, most parents today were raised in blended families. This means both parents were working or they had a single-parent household. Today's parents were raised with either heavy discipline by authoritative parents, or left on their own to work through problems and relied on friends for advice and support. Allow me to expand on how I see this change and the impact it's having on modern families.

What we are doing as a whole is not working for the majority of children.

There has been a major shift in our society in how we raise, treat, and view children. For example, it was not that long ago that most parents expected their children to be obedient, polite, and faithful to church and family. For the most part, these expectations meant children were taught to see and value others, as well as have strong family and community connections. The downside was that there was more of an authoritarian type of interactions adults had with children. Through the years, the self-esteem of the child and child rights became a growing concern. This was, in my opinion, a necessary awareness and did provide positive change. Experts taught that children needed more recognition of self. However, as the next generation of parents sought to right the wrongs done to them under this authoritative parenting style, the pendulum swung toward permissive parenting with a hands-off approach.

I agree that it is psychologically better for people to be empowered, but I also believe that children need to be taught and raised by parents who are intentional and motivated to empower their children in the context of family and community, not just for self. There was a shift in the late 1980s toward a more child-centered parenting approach. The child became the leading focus, and the awareness of others became less valued, if taught at all. Unfortunately, being unbalanced in a self-centered, or "me first" mindset is not always the best way to live in a family or a community. It may be that children became better at expressing themselves, and that was positive. It is also seen as a positive that they learned to choose what they feel is right for themselves and not need parents or adults to tell them what to eat, what to wear, what school to go to, the rules of the games, or the rules of the household. Today, many parents are told that children can make the right choices and decide for themselves about many aspects of their life, and seem to imply that children do not need parents or anyone to be in charge. Yes, we want everyone to feel empowered and confident, however, those who cannot be led also cannot be taught or guided and do not make for great leaders, friends, team players or healthy, happy adults. I do not believe we are seeing better self-expression due to the freedom given to children to make their own decisions and exert their own will, especially at the expense of others within the family.

Society insists that there should be no tension between what we want or need and what others want or need. In many ways, we are told to put ourselves first. However, children who have not encountered a will stronger than their own on a consistent basis develop behavior and patterns of interaction that lead to dysfunction in the home, school, and often in other relationships. Tantrums and manipulation become more powerful, more complex, and much more difficult to handle as the child gets older. This also makes them more susceptible to other emotional difficulties, such as anxiety and depression, and often leads to addiction and personality disorders. Many school-aged children with poor behavior and social skills are improperly diagnosed as emotionally disturbed, oppositionally defiant, or with some other neurological-based conduct disorder, when in fact, the behavior of these children is due to how they are being raised. Even if a child does have ADHD, autism, or any of the most common disorders, parents lack the tools and resources to successfully raise their child and don't understand what a healthy family environment should look like.

A lot of families I work with try very hard to create an environment where their children can talk about their feelings, rules, and consequences, but there are no firm boundaries because they desire to keep things peaceful, open, and full of understanding. I am not against these concepts, but this soft approach often leaves the child alone with his power and without a solid foundation. The child is often quite anxious and insecure, despite grasping for control. When we give power and control before a person is ready, fail to maintain connection, and stop teaching the value of the relationship and consideration of others, the child's character actually gets lost. This is usually when I get called to help the family.

> When we give power and control before a person is ready, fail to maintain connection, and stop teaching the value of the relationship and consideration of others, the child's character actually gets lost.

Many of the families I teach have unhealthy and sometimes unsafe child-rearing methods that don't work with children who are not only strong-willed, but are almost impossible to control. Most of these children struggle with trust and connection, are unable to accept guidance or instruction, and have been used to a high level of power while exhibiting low thresholds for dealing with day-to-day tasks and challenges. Their wants and needs become dominant and are mixed with the desire to control the environment and those in it. When they don't get what they want, they pitch a fit, demand, and argue or simply take what they want. These behavior patterns form the basis for conduct disorders, oppositional defiance, and even attention disorders.

Furthermore, these children become highly anxious and depressed, feeling less and less connected to those around them. This imbalance has generated more personality disorders (especially narcissism) than we've seen in any other generation.

Hopefully it's clear that the shift in how we raise, treat, and view children today has not created the positive change well-meaning parents intended. Instead, children with undeveloped relational skills and character that have not learned to accept leadership create anarchy in the family because they don't have the emotional ability to successfully navigate day-to-day challenges. Additionally, the child fails to mature because of underdeveloped abilities for self-control, emotional regulation, and connection with others. Families have been destabilized by the unbalance of self-will and relational interactions resulting in both adults and children being unhappy and unsettled.

Despite believing "soft parenting" causes more problems than it solves, I don't want the pendulum to swing back to strict authoritative and punitive parenting. Instead, the home should be the central training ground where children are taught the importance of connection and recognition of others instead of selfishness and control. This means parents need to be taught how to be in charge and create structure so that the child can connect, develop, and grow in a healthy manner. We also need to create new models of interactions that establish a balance between power and connection—methods that allow children to recognize and trust adults to be in charge so they can be children and develop healthy relationships within the family. So where do we go from here?

> **The home should be the central training ground where children are taught the importance of connection and recognition of others instead of selfishness and control.**

THE ANSWER IS IN THE HOME

What happens when parents are given the tools they need to successfully raise a child—even if the child has been labeled "difficult"? As I was completing my doctorate studies, my dissertation centered on this question. The answer came from peer-reviewed research papers on programs that focus on a parent-centered approach and from parent surveys from the *Healthy Foundations Family Program*® in Idaho. These results showed that programs and services for children that endeavor to support parents provide many benefits. The benefits included better outcomes for the youth, the parents, and the overall well-being of the family.

One study showed that out-of-home placement, or an over-reliance on out-of-home services, that focus only on the child causes a breakdown in the family.[2] Other research reveals that there is a lack of in-home services available, especially services that focus on helping the parents with the child.[3] Many mental health providers feel pressured to find more restrictive settings for children with emotional or behavioral issues[4]. Sometimes, that pressure comes from the parents who are at the end of their ropes and don't know if it's safe to keep their out-of-control child at home. Unfortunately, any improvements that occur in out-of-home placements tend to be short-lived, with poor behavior returning once the youth is back at home. This is because the parents are not taught the skills needed to deal with the challenges of raising youth with emotional or behavioral disorders. The responsibility falls wholly on the child to utilize skills they learned on their own, which renders the treatment unsustainable outside of the treatment facility.[5]

Research also showed the need to move away from a model of care for children in which professionals work to implement strategies of change with the child while the parents stand by and hope for the best. Instead, professionals need to teach parents to be the experts. They need to provide tools, skills, and therapy that nurtures the family relationship—ideally in the home. This type of service encourages parents to accept responsibility for helping their children tackle life's challenges. Research also shows that parents are critical to children's mental health and necessary for the overall well-being of the child and family.[6] This further validates the importance of programs where professionals treat children in the home and support parents through challenges, rather than only seeing children in clinics and agencies. Additionally, this method supports the parent to develop a more positive and peaceful family environment. When parents are taught new parenting skills, they are better able to support their child and experience positive outcomes. This is especially true if parents can learn these skills and intervene early, when behavioral problems first arise.[7]

Intensive in-home programs, such as the program I designed, address the needs of the families with strong parent support and skill-building in the home environment. Skills learned at home then translate easily to other environments in the community, such as school. Teaching parents to manage their difficulties in the home is the most cost-effective with longer-lasting results. One study pointed out that working in the home with parents creates higher stability because the parents are taught, supported, and encouraged in bringing forth solutions that help promote the child and the family as a whole.[8] I hear this from parents I work with as well. Most of them report that the skills they learned through in-home support helped the most, even if they struggled with the program or didn't see all the changes they hoped to see.

> Professionals need to teach parents to be the experts. They need to provide tools, skills, and therapy that nurtures the family relationship—ideally in the home.

We know that children with behavioral and emotional issues create a great deal of stress in the family and place high demand on the parents. This stress can be extreme and also isolating. In many cases, the family structure and the core relationships are broken because of the turmoil and stress in the household. Providers of intensive in-home programs need to approach families with the understanding that most often, parents of children with Serious Emotional Disturbance (SED) are anxious, overwhelmed, hopeless, feel isolated, and need encouragement and confidence to improve their parenting.[9] Furthermore, research shows that parents' well-being is adversely affected when they are left out of the treatment interventions, when children are placed outside the home, or when they feel unsupported in their efforts.

When parents don't receive support, children who are at risk of being placed outside the home due to behavioral difficulties are more likely to end up in mental hospitals, juvenile courts, and educational alternatives.[10] However, when parents are supported and taught the needed skills, the entire family functions better. Additionally, the parent-child bond is improved because natural design is for children to rely on help from their parents with coping, emotional regulation, problem-solving, and working through a variety of difficulties.[11] When professionals support the parents in teaching and holding appropriate boundaries, creating new patterns of interactions, increasing connectedness, and re-building family structure, parents are able to create a strong family structure, help their children regulate emotions, and create new family dynamics.[12] We must support parents if we as a society, or as professionals, want to help children. Carl Jung stated it well when he said, "If there is anything that we wish to change in a child, we should first examine it and see whether it is not something that could better be changed in ourselves."

TAKEAWAYS

I believe the family is the curative agent for change and that the family itself is foundational to our society. Families are also sometimes the place of the most struggle, hurt, and shame. However, feeling guilty or hopeless because nothing has worked yet isn't going to get you the results you want. Fear and shame hold you back from being the parent you want to be and from creating the family you want to have.

Parents today need a different skillset for parenting. What may have worked for the parent when they were a child is not working now. Today, it seems like our children are larger, stronger, and more self-determined. They are willing to question adults and often come across as entitled as they take what they want from those around them. Therefore, parents need to be prepared for handling more difficult behaviors, which means they also need more support, tools, and resources from professionals.

My passion is teaching parents that they **are** capable of raising "difficult" children who can eventually take their proper place in the family and in society. It's why I created the framework I provide later in this book and teach the tools for parents to succeed. For now, I want you as the parent to know that I respect that you've done the best you can with what you had to work with. This problem has been growing for generations, so it's not your fault, but at the same time it will take you to change it. I want to encourage you to hold on to the hope and truth that it is never too late to turn things around. Even if your child is highly explosive and you are on the verge of needing an outside agency to take over as guardian to your child, there is still hope.

The purpose of the next chapter is to identify some of the executive functioning processes that your child's brain still needs to mature. Gaining this understanding is crucial for you to cultivate compassion towards your child during their challenging moments and to grasp how you can offer them the most effective support. Fortunately, it's not too late and these processes can still be developed, but only if you read on to find out how.

CHAPTER 2

What's Going on in Your Child's Brain?

Disruptive and maladaptive behavior in a child is a symptom that something deeper is going on. Just like a cough may be the result of a virus, poor behavior is also the result of something else. A critical job of a parent is to find out what the issue is behind the behavior of their child. This allows them to bring understanding and support, which aids in helping the child and the family rather than simply treating a symptom. One major cause of challenging behavior is inadequately developed skills the child needs to function better. Understanding what these skills are and how they are developed is key to unlocking the mystery of your child's poor behavior. Before we get into specific executive functioning skills, however, I want you to consider the importance of shifting your perspective from focusing on a symptom to healing the root cause. This shift will help you in supporting and teaching your child rather than punishment or ignoring.

A SHIFT IN PERSPECTIVE

When the oldest two of my six children were about to enter middle school, I began to realize that their behaviors were more than defiance or manipulation. At that time, I was beginning my work with children who had a great many behavioral issues. I learned through training as a behavior intervention specialist that poor behaviors are attempts to communicate the challenges or inner struggles they were experiencing. This new insight began to change my outlook as a parent. I no longer thought of their behaviors as mere defiance or lack of respect; instead, I noticed something more happening beneath the surface of the behaviors. My focus shifted to how I could help my children through the challenges rather than reacting or focusing on how their behaviors seemed to be defying me as the parent. This shift in thinking changed my perspective about others, my children, and even myself. I began thinking more about what they needed or what the cause of the internal struggle might be, rather than just trying to make them stop. I found that even when I felt frustrated, I could ask myself what I needed, or what was so frustrating about the situation and move through the challenge to better outcomes for myself and others. With that newfound understanding came better tools that enabled me to provide help and support rather than just reacting.

> ## Poor behaviors are attempts to communicate the challenges or inner struggles a child is experiencing.

The *Healthy Foundations Family Program*® was developed with the understanding that poor behavior means an inner struggle is happening within the child. Focusing on the behavior is easy, but understanding the struggle behind the behavior is difficult. Our perspective changes as we become curious about what is going on inside a person, instead of focusing on the behavior. For example, sometimes my child would be tired, hungry, frustrated, embarrassed, or disappointed. Knowing and labeling the need allowed me to offer support or meet the need. From there, I was able to help my child articulate their needs instead of displaying defiant behaviors to get their needs met. Doing so raised their self-awareness and helped me to respond in a healthy way.

While it is critical to respond and be aware of the inner struggle, it is important to also remember being tired, hungry, disappointed, sad, or embarrassed is no excuse for poor behavior. I believe that there must be consistent guidelines with our children. The parent's role is to help the child move through their emotions toward a more appropriate and healthy behavior. People are able to work through challenges and we are incredibly resilient.

But children must be taught how to overcome difficulties, especially children that come from complex backgrounds of trauma and abuse. The answer is not ignoring the emotion or dismissing difficult circumstances children may experience; instead, we must be diligent in teaching and supporting them through the challenges while emphasizing standards and guidelines on what is acceptable when strong emotions surface. The following story is an example of how behavior can progress if standards and boundaries are not enforced.

One of my clients had a six-year-old child named Sally. Her mother told me that when she was two, she would scream for what she wanted, throw herself on the ground, and have violent outbursts almost every day. Sally's behavior was dismissed by the mother after being told by friends, family, and her pediatrician that the outbursts were typical for a two-year-old. She was advised to either ignore or distract Sally when she threw a fit to stop the behavior. This seemed to work to a degree, but over time Sally became more demanding. When her mother tried to intervene during a tantrum, Sally would hit, bite, or kick. Often something small would cause a fit, such as buying the wrong cereal. Sally even struggled with friends. Games and activities had to be what Sally wanted. She hated waiting her turn and often changed the rules in any given situation. If the other children got upset, Sally claimed they were being mean to her and that nobody wanted to play with her.

The difficulties continued at school where Sally had trouble getting along with others, following basic instructions and acting out. In first grade, Sally was diagnosed with ADHD, but her mother questioned whether she had a deeper issue. Sally's mom constantly avoided enforcing rules or doing activities Sally didn't like to avoid the tantrums. Her mom struggled to set age-appropriate boundaries because when she did, Sally screamed or pushed back, attempting to fight for control. The "normal" behavior from two-years-old did not resolve on its own; rather, it continued through four, five, and six years old.

Parents today seem to have forgotten that a child pushing boundaries is healthy and natural and not a sign that children need more freedom and less structure. Pushing back is how a child can determine where the boundaries are, but it can also be a way of connecting. By pushing limits and challenging the power of others, a child begins to discover the natural order of their situation and who the trusted leaders are. They come to know where they "rank" in the tribe. But, when the child pushes for control and power and discovers there is no real boundary set, this causes anxiety and insecurity. The result leaves the child needing to control everyone and everything. This is why, even in safe and stable homes, children fighting for control do not feel safe or connected to others around them.

> When a child pushes for control and power and discovers there is no real boundary set, this causes anxiety and insecurity.

There is safety for a child in knowing adults are in control. Unfortunately, as a child's behavior becomes more difficult, parents, caregivers or teachers typically offer less supportive consequences and boundaries weaken. In other words, they back off and require less. Rather than clear, concise instructions and actions, adults tend to focus on the child's emotions and as their behavior becomes more difficult, the adult may be more reactionary, but not really follow through with teaching or upholding consequences that will lead to changes in the behavior. For example, as Sally became more unreasonable, greater effort was put into talking to Sally about her behaviors or reasoning with her on what she was feeling. If she expressed being angry or upset, the school staff would loosen the boundaries and her parents would work harder at trying not to upset her, all of which loosened boundaries and gave her more control. A child who is left alone, empowered to oversee deciding what is right for them apart from adult guidance, creates more anxiety-driven behaviors, which causes more extreme behavior, which leads to more talking and reasoning. It's a vicious cycle.

> There is safety for a child in knowing adults are in control.

Knowing the adults in their life are in control also supports proper development of executive functioning skills, which is a key factor in how a person behaves as they mature. One common dynamic among nearly all children with behavioral problems is that they lack executive functioning skills.

UNDERSTANDING EXECUTIVE FUNCTIONING SKILLS

A challenging child is missing the internal skills necessary for proper executive functioning because the skills were never formed. Brain growth during childhood is vital to the development of executive functioning, but it can be stunted due to early childhood trauma, developmental delays, or lack of care in helping to shape these skills. It's typical for a child who lacks the skills in executive functioning to have difficulty using their knowledge and skills throughout their day. This impacts what we might call their daily performance. The inability to utilize the skills needed leads to frustration in the child and for those around them. The behavior you might notice is more like a toddler, regardless of their age. Please don't mistake this behavior as a lack of intelligence or talent. The child is delayed in the skills to move from outer to inner control and for this reason is often seen as impulsive, hyper, or unable to focus or control themselves.

A person's behaviors are mostly determined by what she or he wants most at any given moment. Inner-control comes from our thought processes, or conscience—it's that little voice in our head that tells us to stop a behavior. Good inner-control can also be seen as self-control. Outer control is how we internalize the influence of someone else, or, how we process family values or societal norms. Children who cannot make good decisions or choose what's right have underdeveloped inner and outer control (executive functioning). Therefore, parents must make choices for the child until he or she is mature enough to do so on their own. This is called external control. External control provides the example for a child to learn how to start processing outer and inner control. Therefore, with external support in place, a child can learn to shift from outer to inner control and perform beyond the delay in development. This shift will not happen on its own.

> Children who cannot make good decisions or choose what's right, have underdeveloped inner and outer control.

According to two major researchers in ADHD and how it is tied into executive functioning, Tom Brown, PhD, and Russel Barkley, PhD, teach that parents and caregivers can help the child improve and balance the impairments by providing longer periods of external support for executive functions. The child must be taught to use knowledge, skills, and abilities as they are guided by external support. This is also true for teenagers. The frontal lobe of the teen brain grows rapidly, which is where executive functioning occurs. For this reason, teens often become more difficult and sometimes unsafe due to their lack of impulse control, good judgment, rational thought processes, and emotional control. But this is no time to give up. They need to be taught to use learned knowledge and skills to help them develop effectively.

An example of how adults use external support on a daily basis is the use of a to-do list. Rather than leaving it up to my working memory to keep track of tasks (an executive function), I use my phone (an external support) for reminders of errands or grocery lists. If I remember my phone, it helps me a lot! Parents need to be the external support as their child develops the skills required to shift to inner control, and can use the skills day to day and in different situations. Think of these missing skills like potholes on a road. You need to go back and fill in the potholes no matter how far down the road you are so that your child can move forward without being handicapped by their missing executive functions.

> Parents need to be the external support as their child develops the skills required to shift to inner control, and can use the skills day to day and in different situations.

The most helpful information for parents of challenging children is a better understanding of executive functioning skills and how they relate to the way these children struggle to function daily. Characteristics of ADHD go beyond attention disorders that make sitting still or paying attention difficult for children. These behaviors involve impairments in executive functioning, which is primary to the development of a person's ability to gain control of themselves and use the skills needed for day-to-day tasks and future development.

Executive functioning includes a distinctive set of mental abilities, or skills. These skills allow a person to direct and regulate their behavior. The prefrontal lobes at the front of the brain perform executive functions. Brain patterns concerning how a person behaves or operates can change throughout a lifetime, which is good news. However, when set or pre-determined patterns are present, intention and support are necessary for positive changes to occur. Take a look at some of the executive functioning skills and think about how these may relate to your child's behavior.

BEHAVIORAL INHIBITION

One of the primary executive functions developed early in life is behavioral inhibition, which is the inner barrier to free activity, expression, or proper functioning. It is what holds us back from acting on something. In highly anxious children, behavioral inhibition can lead to extended periods or patterns of avoidance or insecurity, making transitions and new situations difficult. Inhibition in behavior is necessary as it helps to guard responses or actions before acting them out. It allows us to stop when needed and to resist distractions. Behavioral inhibition lays the foundation for the development of other executive functions, all of which allow for behavioral control.

WORKING MEMORY

Working memory involves using memory to recall events and store the information in your mind to complete a task or activity. Working memory gives you a sense of time, planning, hindsight, reflection, and self-awareness. Consider your child and the frustration you might have with their inability to complete tasks, lack of time management, or how they constantly act before thinking, then forget why they did something.

Perhaps your child has no idea how their actions affect others, or how to shift their attention from one person to another based on who is around. Maybe you have discussed an incident that happened at school and your child seems unwilling to understand, or even remember, what happened and why they got in trouble. Children have told me, "I don't do that anymore" when referring to something they did just the day before!

Working memory is an executive function that allows for self-reflection, insight, and hindsight. Most children struggling with impulse control and delayed gratification need help developing better working memory skills. Once you understand that deficits in working memory affect a person's ability in so many areas, you can help by filling in the blanks for them rather than expecting them to come up with a complete story about what happened, or what went wrong. Don't expect them to be able to tell you what they were thinking before they made the poor decision (that is foresight), or explain in hindsight what they could have done differently. Instead, step in and tell them what you know about what happened and ask if there is anything they would like to add. Then, be direct in how you want them to correct the issue.

INTERNALIZED SPEECH

How does your child handle when they make a mistake or encounter a problem to solve? Many children who struggle to make good choices are not great problem solvers. They make rash and sometimes drastic decisions, get stuck often, or are verbally abusive when talking about themselves, especially if they are stressed or make mistakes. Children with poor executive functioning skills tend to struggle with thinking things through, or going back and correcting poor choices or mistakes. This is all because they lack development of internalized speech.

Internalized speech is when an individual uses self-talk to guide their behavior or thought process. It is the ability to weigh the pros and cons, question yourself, be self-directed, and it helps in solving problems and fixing mistakes. Understanding that your child lacks the ability to have thorough internalized speech should help you respond in ways that offer support in this area of executive functioning.

When your child is struggling to make a decision their stress level is typically quite high, which lowers their ability to process information even further. Limit the choices for them, or simply direct them in what to do. This may sound like, "Since this is a hard choice today, I am going to help you. You can have a cheese stick or an apple for your snack today." When they are less stressed and you have some time, writing down all the pros and cons regarding their options can also be very helpful. Use this to show them how they can pick based on the list.

When they do make a mistake, they may go to a dark place in how they express their regret or embarrassment. This could sound like, "I am so stupid! I never do anything right!" or many other statements of self-hate. Stay calm and don't try to reason with them about why they are not stupid. Be kind and clear with something like, "It's okay to make a mistake. Here's how we fix it." If they are calling themselves names, it is a good time to create a boundary and say, "We don't talk to people that way, that includes ourselves." Or, "Stop being mean. Use kind words."

Again, problem solving is part of internalized speech so realizing that your child is not going to be able to solve something on their own, even if they know the right answer when calm, means they need your help to see their way clearly through it. Ask fewer questions and be clear and direct; this should help develop the next skill, emotional control.

EMOTIONAL CONTROL AND SELF-REGULATION

Your child does not have meltdowns because they think it gets them what they want. They lack the executive functioning skills to control their emotions or respond appropriately. These skills are a function of the brain, not merely a behavioral response.

> Your child does not have meltdowns because they think it gets them what they want. They lack the executive functioning skills to control their emotions or respond appropriately.

Emotional control and self-regulation are the ability to respond fittingly to a situation, especially when it's stressful. They help a person express emotions and facial expressions appropriately. These skills are also associated with self-motivation when starting or completing a task. Self-regulation and motivation also guide us in establishing goals and directing our behaviors to reach those goals. Organizing and planning, developing steps ahead of time, and carrying them out are also associated with self-regulation skills. Your child is going to need you to provide support in some key areas because of these deficits.

Regulation is a critical component of safety and behavioral changes. Chapters Three and Four are dedicated to regulation and safety and they thoroughly explain how you can provide external support, so I won't cover that here. However, I will touch on some emotional control tips to help you now.

Most people, especially children, are not able to make life changes without help. They simply have not had the life experience to be adaptable yet. When your child is losing control of their emotions or has big feelings over seemingly little things, don't try to distract them or talk them out of it. Intervene early; don't wait until they are over-the-top upset. Stay close by, keep them safe, and think about offering support such as, "I can see you are upset, and I am here for you." This doesn't necessarily have to be said, but can be shown through actions as well. Pull them as close as you safely can and support them through the storm of emotions. This can go a long way in working towards regulation and external support. When they see you working with them to solve their problem, it is also an example of how they should work with others.

RECONSTITUTION

Reconstitution is the executive functioning skill needed to work with others in problem-solving and creativity. It involves separating behaviors or ideas and re-assembling them to form new, or creative solutions. Children who struggle with reconstitution tend to feel like everyone is against them. They view it as "mean" if a friend, or group of children, does not play the game they want. They need their ideas to be accepted by everyone else.

You may also notice that your child has difficulty keeping track of time, promptly changing their behavior, focusing, or shifting attention from one task to another. Perhaps they play rough with toys and struggle to regulate their actions. Or maybe they struggle to begin a task, then over-focus on details and cannot complete the task in a timely manner. Multiple skills required on a daily basis are accessed through executive functioning, especially in directing and regulating a person's behavior.

You can provide external support to your child within your family by helping them learn to share ideas, problem solve with siblings, and work through emotions properly. This should be practiced at home so they are more prepared to work with others at school, or on a sports team. Be close by and teach them how to accept others' ideas, opinions, and even change their mind about how to solve a problem rather than expecting that they can do it successfully without help.

A NEW BEGINNING

Hopefully this chapter has helped you understand the importance of developing executive functioning skills and given you some ideas of how your child moves through obstacles, challenges, moods, and behaviors. You might have recognized your child's behaviors in several of the skill explanations above. Understanding their behavior, especially as it relates to a deficiency in the brain, is an important step in helping your child work on the root of the problem instead of reacting to a symptom. Working with your child at the root level also allows compassion and understanding, which your child will notice as well. Use the tips provided here and give the best external support you are capable of providing. It's not too late!

> You can provide external support to your child within your family by helping them learn to share ideas, problem solve with siblings, and work through emotions properly.

TAKEAWAYS

You may have heard the phrase, "You can't teach an old dog new tricks." But, when it comes to the brain and how we function, adapt, and grow, it is never too late to turn things around. Many skills and abilities that require higher executive functioning are taught and developed in early childhood. That said, teens also go through a mental, emotional, and physical growth spurt that is key to frontal lobe development. Unfortunately, these opportunities for growth and development can sometimes be lost for various reasons. When a lack of development can be recognized in a child, regardless of age, the best thing you can do for them, your family, and for society, is provide external support and "catch them up" so they can live their best life. This is the path to a new beginning. Here are a few other key takeaways from this chapter:

1. Disruptive and maladaptive behavior in a child is a symptom of an underlying issue. It is important for parents to shift their perspective from focusing on the behavior to understanding and addressing the root cause of the behavior.

2. Challenging behavior in children can be caused by inadequately developed executive functioning skills. Understanding these skills and how they are developed is crucial in helping children improve their behavior and functioning.

3. External support and guidance are essential for children with executive functioning deficits. Parents need to provide consistent boundaries, guidelines, and consequences while helping their child develop inner control and self-regulation.

4. Behavioral inhibition, working memory, internalized speech, emotional control, and reconstitution are key executive functioning skills that impact a child's behavior and daily functioning. Recognizing deficits in these areas can help parents provide targeted support and interventions.

Next, I want to discuss the level beyond a "challenging" child—the highly frustrated and inflexible child. Children at this level are quite volatile and can escalate to anger and violence quickly. Even if your child hasn't reached this level, don't skip the next chapter because the concepts and skills apply at all levels. Turn the page to discover three amazing tools for dealing with any child in an aggravated situation.

CHAPTER 3

Highly Frustrated and Inflexible

Most of the homes I enter are described by the parents as chaotic, crazy, full of conflict, in turmoil, and in crisis mode all the time. They typically have children that are angry, defiant, aggressive, and willful. They will argue all day long about even the most basic things. This has become "normal" for me to work with. However, over the years I have seen a growing number of children who are more and more violent and increasingly more destructive in their explosive episodes. Their parents are worn out, there are high amounts of tension, doors are broken, and there are holes in the walls. It's not uncommon for calls to the police to end up in detention or mental hospital stays. Parents report they don't feel safe at home and are not able to keep the other children in the family safe. This is the highest level of concern as the next step is usually an out-of-home placement.

I wanted to address this "extreme" in behaviors early on so you can know that positive changes can occur, even in the toughest of situations. Plus, if you can understand some of the explosiveness of this type of child, you can learn that they will need consistent training in very specific areas, over and over until they get it. While I start by providing a general overview of the typical explosive child, keep in mind that these characteristics are common among most difficult children, just to a lesser degree. Next, I'll discuss how to keep yourself emotionally regulated so you can keep calm even when your child may be starting to lose control. I'll also explain how to use the Mountain of Escalation as a tool to determine the agitation level of your child. Finally, I'll explain the Calm+5 exercise, which is a great transition to moving on with your day after your child escalates behavior. This is a longer chapter, but it's packed full of useful guidance and tools to help with your child … explosive or not.

IT'S NOT INTENTIONAL

I find it helpful to understand that children who explode easily and intensely do not choose to act this way. Rather, they have difficulty in problem-solving, planning, organizing their thoughts, and controlling their impulses. These are all skills that need to be taught. I have found that the more explosive children really struggle with applying these skills when they need them the most, so their behavior is not planned or intentional. We need to help children manage their frustration rather than having a dramatic negative reaction.

It may also help if you understand that once a child is frustrated or escalated for any reason, they will struggle to think clearly, or process your guidance. Therefore, it is important for them to be taught over and over to get calm enough to reason, problem-solve, organize their thoughts, and control their impulses. These skills are not easy for them as they tend to be inflexible and highly irrational over minor issues. This often causes the people around them to act in similar ways, with knee-jerk reactions. Instead, parents need to be able to stay calm so they can teach, connect, and help their children stay in their right mind to work through frustrations.

SELF-REGULATE BEFORE TRYING TO CO-REGULATE

When your child escalates their behavior and becomes annoying or defiant, it is important to recognize that your system is also getting dysregulated and requires some calming strategies in order to help your child to get calm. I totally understand this can be a challenge when your child is acting out, attacking you, or being destructive and defiant—especially if explosive behavior has been the norm in your house for any period of time. Understand that learning to regulate yourself will take a little time to master, but it is necessary. You must get yourself calm so that you can be solid and stable for your child. As you begin to respond, rather than react, and as you allow yourself to calm, your child's brain will mirror yours. You cannot demand that your child get calm. They need to co-regulate with you.

Co-regulation works, but it must start with the sanest person in the room getting calm first. Remember, your child doesn't have the same processing skills as you, so you have to model what getting calm looks like to help them manage theirs. Instead of yelling, threatening, bribing, ignoring, giving in, belittling, punishing or trying to win the battle, think about them using your presence to mirror your brain in gaining self-control and regulation. Sometimes I ask parents to think about how they can take a step back from the situation, without just leaving or isolating themselves or the children. Usually this involves the parent being quiet, more talking seems to escalate both the parent and child. Be there, and use simple phrases we will teach in the connecting part of this book, but let your words be few, quiet, and calm while you work on breathing and getting calm. I also ask that they consider working on lowering their heart rate and strive to be the lowest heart rate in the room. But how do you get calm?

> **Understand that learning to regulate yourself will take a little time to master, but it is necessary.**

The first step to regulating yourself and getting calm is to identify the emotions you are feeling. Is this situation stressful? Are you feeling hurt, angry, frustrated, or discouraged? Many times, the process of trying to identify your specific emotion is enough to start your own regulation process. Acknowledging that this is hard, or that you are frustrated to yourself seems silly, but it is very grounding, and it helps. I put my hand on my chest and say in a whisper, "Wow, this is hard. I am feeling totally frustrated right now." It gives the emotion the attention it needs while keeping your executive functioning available enough to not camp out in those feelings. Acknowledge the feelings and know it is okay to have them. Once you have identified your emotions, work to let them pass without taking hold of you or your actions, to allow yourself to calm down further. You don't need to shout your frustration at everyone in the house, but you do need to recognize what you are feeling and if you are getting overwhelmed. Breathwork is a great way to achieve this step.

Breathing. I don't tell children to breathe. Instead, I first make sure I am taking deep breaths, inhaling for several seconds and holding, then exhaling for several seconds. Take a breath instead of answering an insult or reacting to what the child is doing. Remember, the child's brain will take over if it has another person to copy in the moment. Be mindful of yourself and your tension. Again, think about being the lowest heart rate in the room and getting yourself as calm as you can. Keep your responses predictable and calm as well. Encourage your child through your responses rather than controlling them with your reactions. Once you have control of your breath and feel calm, continue providing guidance to your child. If the situation has escalated beyond a simple breathing exercise, or you don't feel yourself getting calmer, don't hesitate to take a time out.

> Encourage your child through your responses rather than controlling them with reactions.

Take a time out. In the heat of the moment, you may need a break. This is what reasonable people can recognize and do when their own emotions are running high. Eventually, your child will be able to ask for a break as well. But first you need to practice and model it in healthy ways.

The break must be short and intentional. For example, if your child was arguing and defiant in the kitchen, then they get upset, run to their room, slam their door and maybe even swear at you a bit. Don't rush after them or demand they come back out. Take a break. You may need to do some breathwork first before you can address them in a calm way, so take a minute or two to self-regulate. Then, go to the room and tell him, "I need a break and I think you do too. I will check back with you in ten minutes." Then set the timer, stay close by and use that ten minutes to get yourself fully calm and present. Then go by the door and let him know, "I am right here, when you are ready, please sit on the couch. (or bed or floor)."

If you leave for too long, most children will stay elevated and begin to do things to get you reengaged in the battle. As your child learns to self-regulate a bit, they may be able to handle being alone in their room and calm down. But for now, stay close. Set the timer and let them know once the timer goes off, they need to come out of the room and together you can finish what was started. Remember, this is a time out for the parent, not the child. Later in this chapter I will explain the Calm+5 exercise, which is a great way to transition a child from an escalated state to continuing with the activities of the day.

Another way a parent can take a break is from the constant chatter and demand of your attention. If you feel yourself getting dysregulated while your child talks to you, or due to how they are answering questions, quickly give yourself a time out from listening. You can stay nearby, but direct the child to sit at a table or on the couch with an activity. Tell them is it quiet time and you are taking a break from listening and talking while they work on an activity (reading, drawing, journal, etc.). Be sure to set clear expectations as well. "The next twenty minutes is quiet play and no one is talking. I am setting the timer now." You could also say, "I want to hear more about this, but right now let's do this task without talking." Or, "I can't talk about this anymore right now. Let's take a break and talk later."

Shape Your Perspective: One thing I find particularly helpful is to remember that my primary role as a parent/caregiver is to teach my child the skills needed to overcome their current challenges. It always helps me calm down when I can remember my larger purpose in the relationship. Here are some things to ask/tell yourself that can help you gain perspective and stay in control:

- How can I model calm for her?
- He needs me to show him how to breathe and get control.
- We are working through hard things. It will get better.
- I will never give up no matter how hard it becomes.
- What do I need to do to create safety in this moment?
- He is struggling and I can help by being here for him.
- How can I be clear about what I want her to do instead of what I want her to stop doing?
- Take a breath and just be here right now.

Remember, you cannot talk someone into calming down. However, through talking, venting, releasing tension, movement, or even anger, people can get calmer and usually do so if there is someone present acting as an anchor during their storm. Hold the safety boundaries, know your limits, and work on being the calmest in the room.

WHAT SKILLS ARE NEEDED?

Typically, highly frustrated children have very little insight about themselves. They may come off as demanding, self-centered, or lacking empathy or social tact. They appear to not get along with others, but they are actually unskilled and need to be taught how. Additionally, they are unskilled in recognizing how they feel and how their behavior impacts others. Highly frustrated children need to be taught to say, "I don't know what to do." Or, "I need help." Or, "This is bothering me." Your child lacks experience using a different approach to things that are difficult, annoying, or that challenge their immediate want or perceived need. Because they don't have the skills to deal with these elements of life, they tend to wrap everything in anger.

Fear and anger drive behaviors, and anger often gets wrapped around other emotions that may be harder to express. For example, if your child is embarrassed, hurt, sad, lonely, or disappointed, anger is likely to be seen. These other emotions feel less powerful, and anger is strong in the face of the less desirable emotions. You may have to learn to read between the lines, knowing that they don't have the appropriate words or skills to handle most feelings on their own. Therefore, phrases like, "I hate you!" or, "Screw this!" could just as well be, "I'm hungry" or "I'm bored." Help them pay attention to their emotions as the difficulty arises. These types of skills are rarely taught by just talking about the need for them and should be demonstrated whenever possible.

Children who are highly explosive also lack skills in flexibility and handling frustration. These are critical skills that cannot be forced, rather they need to be modeled and taught. Your reaction to their inflexibility and frustration is also critical. Both children and adults need to stay rational when frustrated. For you as a parent, it means you will need to respond or intervene early, before they are at their worst. Catch their frustration before it reaches the tipping point, and move forward to help, redirect or acknowledge. Don't wait to see if they will work it out, your child cannot handle it … yet. If you become more inflexible and frustrated as the caregiver, a meltdown is sure to happen. So, take notice of their degree of frustration and keep in mind that we need to help them work through it. The most effective tool we have found and use in the *Healthy Foundations Family Program®* is the Mountain of Escalation.

MOUNTAIN OF ESCALATION

One of the most successful ways to keep a child from reaching an explosive level is by recognizing signs of escalation as early as possible. Once you are familiar with their signs of frustration and the patterns of how they react to hard situations, you can take more appropriate action to co-regulate their system, provide guidance, and teach coping skills before their emotions get out of hand. At Healthy Foundations, we use a tool called the Mountain of Escalation that helps parents determine where their child is emotionally at any given time. Knowing their escalation level allows the parents to also choose the best way to intervene. It is imperative for parents of highly frustrated and irrational children to know where they are on the mountain at all times. You might be thinking this is a bit much, but if your child ramps up from zero to sixty in a nanosecond, then you need to have this awareness at *all* times.

The goal is to intervene early. Interventions with a child who is losing control may look different at different levels of their escalation. Redirection (not bribes or threats), moving in closer, making a suggestion, or setting a limit are examples of interventions that can be helpful at lower levels. These are positive and direct actions that help the child feel reassured, connected, and safe. Further up the mountain, reducing tension and maintaining safety become more critical, so it's good to know where the transitions happen. The image below shows the stages of escalation and is a very useful reminder for parents when they are learning their child's warning signs.

You can print a copy of this chart at www.healthyfoundations.com/book-resources. Hang it wherever makes sense for you and your family so you don't need to remember everything as things get heated. Now, let's take a look at the lowest level, Baseline Calm.

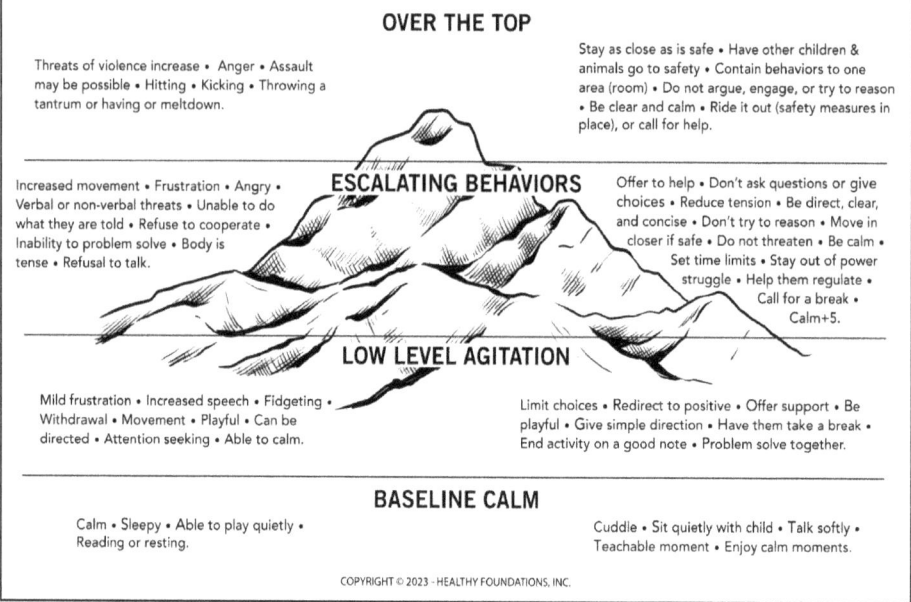

LEVEL 1 - BASELINE CALM

The lowest level of the mountain is what I call Baseline Calm. For most parents of difficult children, and especially parents with highly frustrated children, this may be a rare sight. If you do recognize your child being calm, able to play quietly, reading, or resting, this is simply a moment to enjoy. Grab a cuddle, talk softly with them, capitalize on a teachable moment, or find a way to connect with your child and build a deeper bond.

Unfortunately, most children who have a trauma history, mood disorders, and even ADHD do not hang out around the baseline long, if at all. Even their resting heart rate may be faster than the typical child. So, when you think your child escalates from baseline to the top in no time at all, they may be operating most days well above the baseline already. The next level above baseline is, Low Level Agitation.

LEVEL 2 - LOW LEVEL AGITATION

Mild frustration • Increased speech • Fidgeting • Withdrawal • Movement • Playful • Can be directed • Attention seeking • Able to calm.

Limit choices • Redirect to positive • Offer support • Be playful • Give simple direction • Have them take a break • End activity on a good note • Problem solve together.

Child Actions: Children with low level agitation are just starting to display their frustration. They may not be fully angry yet, but they will display some signs that it is progressing in that direction. You may notice your child starting to talk a lot, louder or faster. They may start moving around more or pacing a little. Sometimes, they start touching things they are not supposed to, almost like they are asking for trouble. You may notice that you are repeating yourself because they keep doing the thing you told them to stop doing. Some children may start to shut down, move slower, withdraw, and talk less, so keeping them present is more of a challenge here.

I also see a lot of mildly agitated children grab something with sugar—candy, cookies, a fruit drink or soda, or something they know they are not allowed to have. They may start to seek attention, but should be able to follow simple instructions given in a clear and concise manner. Seeking attention may be in a negative form, like pushing buttons of family members and being annoying. The higher they are at this level, the less likely they will be to follow directions, ask for help or settle into an activity.

> I see a lot of mildly agitated children grab something with sugar—candy, cookies, a fruit drink or soda, or something they know they are not allowed to have.

Some children do need a little time and space at this level, but may not be able to ask for it. If you notice this, say, "Why don't you take a break and in ten minutes we will have a snack (or play a game, or whatever is next on the schedule)." A break can be as simple as going to wash their hands and face, getting a drink of water, using the bathroom, putting something away in their room, or switching activities all together. It is not a time out; it is a re-direction so that we can move on or reset. Eventually, we want the children to be able to tell us what they need at this level, but they aren't there yet.

Parent Response: A key in early intervention is to remember that the more out of control someone is of their body (including their mouth), the more they need external control, guidance, or help to be safe. Your child also needs to understand they can be allowed freedom of movement and space if they can be safe and in control. Move in closer in a non-threatening way when you see them escalating. Sometimes it is enough to change where they are sitting, or to sit by them at these lower levels and simply offer support.

The Low Level Agitation stage is not a good time for teachable moments, but it is okay to problem-solve. Be a good listener and try to identify the emotion behind what your child is saying so you can help them process what they feel and understand what is agitating them. When asking questions, focus on solutions rather than their emotions. Instead of asking, "How do you feel about _____?" Try, "What can we do about _____?" Ultimately, don't push too hard to find out what is going on. Instead, deal with what you have. At this level, if you are able to redirect into an activity, you can also find connection, which might even allow you to talk about what is going on for them or how you can help them turn it around.

> A key in early intervention is that the more out of control someone is of their body (including their mouth), the more they need external control, guidance, or help to be safe.

Another effective intervention at this stage is to have your child move into a different activity—a game, an art project, or even a movement exercise. Move with them as you provide this redirection and keep an attitude of, "Let's go do …" rather than, "You need to calm down and go do _____." You could also offer a break from the agitating situation to shift the momentum. You might point out, "It looks like you are getting frustrated with this, can you continue or do we need to take a break?" If they refuse the break and continue to be upset, or look like they might blow up, be more direct. "We will come back to this. Let's work on _____ instead."

Finally, it's also helpful at this level to limit choices rather than leaving options open-ended. I have found challenging children get anxious with too many options. For example, instead of asking, "What would you like for a snack?" Limit the options with, "Would you like fruit or cheese for a snack?" Toward the upper end of this stage, it may be helpful to remove choices altogether and limit questions to a minimum. The snack example above would become, "Let's have a snack. I'll make you peanut butter and crackers."

LEVEL 3 - ESCALATING BEHAVIORS

Child Actions: As your child moves up the mountain to the next level, try to remember that they are also losing control of their reactions and thought processes. This means you will need to talk less and be very clear with your directions and instructions.

You may notice your child getting angry, or reaching levels of frustration that could easily get out of hand. Be aware that some children do okay pacing and muttering, even stomping around, while other children will continue to ramp up, break things, or get more aggressive if they are not contained in some way. Stay close enough to be engaged and present, but not in range to get hurt or engaged in a power struggle or the argument.

A child at this level may also start to threaten you or others in the family. Threats may be verbal or nonverbal, depending on the child, so don't mistake silence as being in control. Try to notice if the child's body is tense, or if they seem to no longer be able to solve problems. At this stage, the child is also typically unable to do what they are told and refuses to cooperate.

While you need to help them reduce tension, you cannot do it by walking on eggshells, talking them out of it, or punishing them for how they are acting. Stay firm, remain calm, and be the authority they need you to be in this moment.

Parent Response: At the Escalating Behaviors stage, it is no longer advantageous to give choices to your child. You have to make the call on what you want them to do, when, and where. This level is also where you need to be calm, consistent, stay out of the power struggle, and hold firm to a single requirement—usually to release tension and calm down. Don't bring in all the things that are happening or how they have been acting this way all morning. Yes, they have a bad attitude, but are they able to listen to what you said to do and are doing it (even if it is irritating)?

At this level, don't put yourself in harm's way. Create a way to contain their release of tension, and move on. Some parents might require that the child be in their room. Others may want their child to sit at the table or come stand by the parent (assuming it is safe to do so). If your child is angry and upset in their room, make sure they know you are close by and that you are waiting until they are calm enough to move on. Your child will be a little lower on the mountain after releasing some tension, but not usually at baseline. So, don't try to teach or preach or give consequences at this time. Move forward and continue with your day.

Don't try to talk them out of their mood. But do be clear that you are waiting and when they are able to be calm, we will move on with the day. Most children at this level are able to calm down but you need to know it will take about twenty minutes before they are ready to start something like the Calm+5 exercise. Do not cut corners just because they calmed down enough to come out of their room, or stop shouting.

OVER THE TOP

OVER THE TOP

Threats of violence increase • Anger • Assault may be possible • Hitting • Kicking • Throwing a tantrum or having or meltdown.

Stay as close as is safe • Have other children & animals go to safety • Contain behaviors to one area (room) • Do not argue, engage, or try to reason • Be clear and calm • Ride it out (safety measures in place), or call for help.

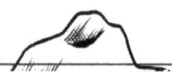

Child Actions: If your child continues to escalate, or they are in a state where people or things are getting destroyed, they have reached the top of the mountain. Verbal abuse and physical assault are definitely possible, as are massive tantrums and meltdowns.

Parent Response: At this point, your child is releasing tension in a negative and destructive way, so activate your safety plan and do what you can to contain the behaviors to one area. Be clear, calm, and do not argue or try to reason with your child. If it seems that others may be in danger, have other children and animals go to a safe place.

Ride out the storm the best you can if you know you can make it over the mountain. Otherwise, do not hesitate to call for help if needed. Some children will run out of the house, hurt everyone in their path, and refuse to go to a safe place to cool off. In this situation, you may have to call the police. Once you make it through the crisis, you will want to do the Calm+5 and then move forward with your day. If the explosion happens in the evening, bedtime is a good idea!

THE CALM+5 EXERCISE

Calm+5 is a calming exercise for regulating emotions, keeping a child safe during a meltdown, and for connection. It is NOT used as punishment, time out, restraint, or for correction purposes. How close the child is to you in a Calm+5 will depend largely on the needs of the child, the issue around safety, and the ability of the parent to avoid power struggles and keep the child safe. The Calm+5 is a tool for you and your child to regulate together. It will not work for you to tell your child to do a Calm+5 or send them away from you to get regulated. The goal with Calm+5 is for the child to be able to get calm with the parent, and then to stay calm and relaxed with the parent for five minutes, reconnect, and then be able to be redirected by the parent. How long this takes will depend on the child. I tell children it can last five minutes (hardly ever) or it can take all day. You as the parent are committed to seeing it through.

The idea behind the Calm+5 is that when a person is struggling (and I encourage you to see your child as struggling) you must act as their solid object and allow that person to hold on to something calmer and more stable than they are. As the anchor in the crisis, I need you to be calm, unafraid, and able to stay centered, balanced, and empathetic. When you catch a crisis in the early stages, or when the child has learned to calm themselves, you can direct the child to come sit by you, or to sit on the couch and you will sit close by. You can also have the child stand by you—

whatever makes the most sense in the moment. This is NOT a time for talking or lecturing, but just a chance to get calm so you can redirect the energy. If and when things escalate, use the Calm+5 to keep your child safe. You can do this by sitting close to your child with your arms around them, or by sitting nearby if they are in their room (or under their bed). For youth who are very aggressive and violent, a safety hold taught by a professional is the best answer to let the child know you can and will keep them safe. Unfortunately, I cannot teach that type of hold in this book.

It is imperative that you use the Calm+5 correctly. You must have your child be calm for the designated amount of time. Before the timer can start, they must be sitting or lying down without wiggling, talking, or fidgeting. If you are staying close, you will notice when their body relaxes, so you don't have to ask, "Are you ready?" You will also need to be calm, and for the most part, you should be quiet as well. You can reassure your child with simple phrases such as, "It's okay, I've got you." Or, "Quiet your body and then we can start the timer." No explanations or corrections for the behavior should be given. The child is linked to you for safety reasons. You may spend a lot of time the first few weeks working on this. Trust the process! It will work. You and your child will be amazed at their ability to get themselves calmed down and ready to move forward.

TAKEAWAYS

The primary focus of this chapter was to provide some insight for parents of highly frustrated and inflexible children. The main thing I want parents to learn is that your child is not intentionally being aggressive, angry, and violent. They literally don't have the skills needed to cope in many situations we would consider normal, to slightly agitating. Because they don't have the skills, parents need to understand their role is to stay calm, keep their child safe, and teach the needed skills at appropriate times.

One important skill most parents need to learn is to regulate their own emotions before attempting to co-regulate with their child. By using techniques such as deep breathing, taking a break, and shifting their perspective, parents can model calmness and provide a stable anchor during their child's emotional storms.

Another key takeaway is to know where your child is emotionally on the Mountain of Escalation at all times. Understanding a child's escalation level allows you to intervene early and provide the necessary support to keep your child from escalating further up the mountain. Don't forget to print out a copy of the Mountain of Escalation from www.healthyfoundations.com/book-resources, then hang a copy wherever you may need to reference it.

Finally, the Calm+5 exercise is a tool you will use over and over to help your child regulate emotions, ensure safety during meltdowns, and foster connection. The goal is for the child to achieve calmness, spend five minutes in that state, reconnect with the parent, and then be redirected to continue with the day.

Self-regulation, the Mountain of Escalation, and Calm+5 will all be critical to your success in building a bridge to the family you want. Start practicing these now, even before you finish this book. The next chapter goes deep into creating safety in the home, which may be the most important stone in the whole bridge. Without safety, nothing else can move forward. Turn the page and learn how to put this vital stone in place!

CHAPTER 4

Safety

Do you want your child to trust you and feel loved? Do you long for a connection with your child that brings your family closer together? It may seem like these feelings are impossible right now, and I totally appreciate your position. Children who have experienced trauma, struggle with attachment, or who are missing executive functioning skills may not develop trust, feel safe, or understand love and security as we do. Plus, attachment and connection can be challenging as well. This means trust, love, and connection must be strategically developed in order to bridge the gap between where your child is now, and where you want them to be.

Several stones are required to move from challenging to healthy behaviors, including safety, structure, regulation, connection, and awareness. However, safety is the most important to establish first and must be achieved in the home before any of the others can be enjoyed. Safety is foremost in the work that lies ahead and must be woven throughout each stone of the bridge as you move into a better future with your family. Your child must feel safe before they can learn to trust. And they must trust you in order to feel love and connection.

In this chapter, I will focus on why safety is such an important stone for bridging the gap and how you can create a safe environment for your child and family. I will teach you two new tools, the three-foot rule and the schedule, which are essential elements that allow you to closely supervise your child and provide much needed structure. You will also start to notice how these new tools work together with what you learned in the last chapter, enhancing your use of the Mountain of Escalation and the Calm+5 exercise. I'm sure you're getting excited and more than ready to create a safe home, so let's get started!

SAFETY

Safety is the action word for love. It says to the child, "I can take care of you and you are not too difficult to handle, even when you push me." Imagine that you needed to change a light bulb and the only way you could reach it was to stand on a table. You might push and wiggle the table to see if it is strong enough to support you. If it feels unstable, or not strong enough to keep you safe, you may keep pushing it around and testing it to see if it will be up for the challenge. But until it demonstrates that it can support your weight, you won't trust it to keep you safe. In the same way, your role as the parent is to be your child's stable object who is strong enough to keep them safe—even when they are violent, aggressive, or pushing you away.

Obvious examples of safety concerns are when a child has major outbursts, hurts others or themselves, refuses to listen, acts impulsively and is disruptive, or disregards rules and boundaries. A child that is out of control, making threats to others or of self-harm, does not feel safe—even inside themselves.

Safety is the action-word for love.

No matter how they try to prove that you can't handle them, you must stand firm through their pushing and testing. This requires a loving, but consistent and firm approach. You need to prove to your child that safety is primary in your home and that you will not only keep them safe, but will not give up on them. Watching this repeated demonstration of maintaining safety will give them a better understanding of love, connection, and the security of meaningful relationships. As I mentioned before, safety is the stone that must be established first. However, there are elements of connection that are useful to establishing safety, so I'll discuss those now.

CONNECTION STRENGTHENS SAFETY

Connecting with a difficult child is not easy! It is especially challenging when they exhibit unsafe or hurtful behaviors. But connection is essential to creating safety, particularly within the family as this is where the child typically learns proper interactions with others.

Developing safe, healthy relationships within the family are a super important part of connection. They are the first relationships that a child forms, lay the foundation for all future relationships in a person's life, and give the child a sense of belonging that they won't get anywhere else. Furthermore, a safe, healthy relationship forms a connection to the parent as the teacher, protector, and authority. Babies are born with a natural connection to their mothers. However, even in biological families, parents need to teach toddlers how to work within the family dynamic. Toddlers must be taught proper behavioral responses and appropriate daily social skills within the family. This creates a connection with siblings and forms the foundation of proper behavior they will use later among peers. Ultimately, stronger relationships in the child's family life enables them to function better outside the home. While connecting with your child may be your goal, the real deal for the child is to feel safe, which requires trust. Repeated demonstrations that you care about the child are essential for building trust.

INCREASE SAFETY BY DEMONSTRATING YOU CARE

Care is another action word for love. Parents can show children they care by establishing firm and consistent boundaries and structure in the home. Doing so says to the child, "I care too much about you to allow you to continue unhealthy behaviors." Setting boundaries and creating structure is not just about restricting the child's activities, nor should it come from fear-based parenting or a punitive model that promotes a child's failure. Their purpose is to ensure everyone in the home feels cared for and safe.

The other way to show you care is to maintain a close, physical presence, serving as the stable object for your child, especially when bad behavior crops up. This demonstrates that you will not leave the child to calm themselves down or handle their emotions alone. Instead, you are there walking beside them, teaching them how to connect, communicate, and be part of the family. Consistently being there for them also reinforces that you won't give up on them, and that you will continue teaching and re-teaching them until they are able to do so on their own. This repeated demonstration builds more trust and connection, therefore increasing safety for all.

> Parents can show children they care by establishing firm and consistent boundaries and structure in the home.

I will go deeper into connection in a future chapter as it is one of the main stones. However, creating boundaries and structure, developing strong family relationships, and showing how much you care are the most important elements of connection that are required for safety. Despite having this knowledge, I would be doing a disservice to parents if I didn't acknowledge that there can be barriers that challenge your will, beliefs, or abilities.

BARRIERS TO CREATING SAFETY

You Are in Charge. Many parents struggle believing they should take charge, or may not understand how to do so. It may even feel silly to say, "I am in charge!" Yet, parents taking charge sets the foundation that promotes healthy brain pathways and behaviors in the child. You can see this in the child who is running the show at home. They don't feel safe, so they are trying to find safety by being in control. When parents create boundaries and structure, however, the child will test or fight against them. This normal order of authority encourages the child's executive functioning to mature.

Of course, there are better ways to take charge than others. Some parents take charge with a drill sergeant mentality—yelling that they are in charge and often getting louder and more physical to demonstrate this. Other parents shy away from being in charge because they fear becoming the drill sergeant parent. Either way, fear is the basis behind both options. Fear of losing control causes the parent to strive for control through authoritarian or overly harsh, strict parenting. On the flip side, fear of being too harsh causes the parent to adopt an overly permissive style, simply hoping to avoid conflict. This gives the parent a false sense of safety and control. Allowing fear to drive your parenting style also reduces your ability to establish stability and safety. The good news is, as you begin to use the tools in this book those fears will diminish and you will develop more confidence as the parent in charge. This, in turn, creates more security and trust for you from your children.

Keep Calm and Parent On. Another barrier to creating safety is getting angry and frustrated at your child. Though anger and frustration may be warranted, these emotions do not help establish stability or safety in the home. In fact, they usually have the opposite effect, creating more distrust and struggle for control.

Anger and frustration keep you from responding appropriately in any given situation. When children are angry and unsafe, or even just annoying, you must maintain calm to show your child what it looks like. You need to model the behavior you want to see. The best way to de-escalate a situation is to catch it early. Noticing when your child is getting angry and their behavior is escalating is essential in understanding the way you should respond. The Mountain of Escalation diagram provided in Chapter Three will help you identify how agitated your child is and equip you to respond appropriately.

Lose Sight—Lose the Fight. Difficult children require constant attention to maintain safety. I put this in the "barriers" section because I know how hard keeping constant awareness of your child can be. That said, I want to stress how important it really is to strive for this.

Challenging kids have a propensity to get in the most trouble when out of the parent's line of sight. So, increase safety in your home by keeping the challenging child close to you with increased watchfulness. Doing so ensures that no harm comes to the child and sends the message that you care enough, and are strong enough to keep them safe. Your presence as a parent is powerful. One tool that I teach all of the families I work with to help with this barrier is the three-foot rule.

THE THREE-FOOT RULE

Parents often say that something always goes wrong if they leave their child alone, even for a short time. But challenging children can't be left alone—

especially when they are agitated or greatly upset. Sending them to their room to get calm, do a task, or play after they have escalated usually results in holes in the wall, broken toys, or worse. They don't have the focus to comply with tasks when left alone and can get distracted from something as simple as brushing their teeth. When agitated, part of their calming down process might be to break things and scream curse words, so trusting them to go off on their own is not the best idea. For these reasons, the three-foot rule is an imperative tool for creating safety in the home and provides the parent guidelines to follow in what seems like an impossible task.

The three-foot rule is exactly what it sounds like—you must keep your child within a three-foot radius of you, while keeping siblings and peers outside of three feet. This is approximately an arm's length away. When a person is upset or angry, staying three feet away is respectful of their personal space, yet allows for near immediate intervention if necessary. The closeness provides time and room for the best opportunities for connection and understanding. You will also have significantly increased awareness of where your child is on the Mountain of Escalation, allowing for timely and appropriate intervention.

> The three-foot rule is exactly what it sounds like—you must keep your child within a three-foot radius of you, while keeping siblings and peers outside of three feet.

You may already be thinking that the three-foot rule won't be possible for you to utilize, especially if you have multiple kids. However, kids adjust quickly to the three-foot rule, even in larger families. With more kids, it's best to keep them all within your line of sight instead of within three feet. Also, limit interactions when kids are closer than three feet. The child who instigates problems or struggles the most needs to be closest to you and farthest from siblings.

It will also help your sanity to schedule downtime and playtime where the child is within your line of sight, but outside of three feet. However, the more intentional you are at staying close, the greater results you will see. As an example of the usefulness of this tool, and to encourage you to use it even if you don't think it seems possible, I have provided a case study at the end of this chapter about one of my more challenging clients, Lucas. His behavior was terrorizing and he got into the most trouble when left alone. The three-foot rule changed everything in the home for him and his mother.

You should also keep in mind that you won't need to use the three-foot rule forever. As you teach your child good behavior, model proper social interactions, and when violence has been eliminated, you should be able to relax this rule more and more. This tool is for helping to restore relationships and interactions. As the family heals and becomes more cohesive, interactions improve, and the three-foot rule and constant supervision may only be needed occasionally. I totally understand that this isn't necessarily a "convenient" way to go through your day. But you aren't reading this book for convenience. You are reading it to learn the tools and structure necessary to have the family you know you deserve. Extreme situations require extreme measures, but I know you can do it, especially when you add the next tool to your toolbox: creating a clear and visual schedule.

THE SCHEDULE

Providing a schedule of what is happening throughout the day for your child to see may not seem like an obvious tool to generate safety, but it is very important. Producing and posting a visible schedule lets the child know that you are monitoring them closely and establishing safety in the home. It also sends the message, "I've got everything in control." Even if you face a crisis and don't know what to do in the moment, the schedule makes it appear that you have a handle on things. Plus, since adults rely mostly on verbal communication and often change their plans, having a visual schedule also holds you accountable and helps you maintain consistency. By taking charge and directing the day, you give your child a chance to be a child because they don't have to think about what to do and how to manage others in the environment.

Do not make the schedule about a list of tasks to complete. It needs to focus on routines and center around the family. I recommend writing the daily schedule on a large whiteboard, including thirty-minute increments of activities from the time the child wakes up until they go to bed. Another thing I recommend is to list all of the known parts of the day first. For example, morning and bedtime routines, meal and snack times, and routines for before and after school should all be listed first. Normal routines may change on non-school days, but it will help build good habits around difficult parts of the day if you keep the schedule fairly consistent. It may also help to pair preferred activities with non-preferred ones. For example, clean-up time is scheduled right before a snack, or getting ready for bed is done before family reading time. A more flexible example is to require two chores to be completed before family game time is allowed.

> Do not make the schedule about a list of tasks to complete. It needs to focus on routines and center around the family.

Consider the schedule a working document and don't be afraid to make changes if needed. You may find that some parts of the day are particularly difficult, so consider cutting back on the number of tasks to be completed. For instance, if mornings are always difficult, there may be too much in the routine that is getting in the way of waking up, getting dressed, eating, and getting out the door. Keep it simple. You will settle into a flow fairly quickly based on your family's needs.

Be sure to add downtime, especially on non-school days. Early in the program, I recommend thirty minutes of downtime in the morning and afternoon. Or you may add an hour in the afternoon if there is no time in the morning. Downtime should be limited because kids with challenges tend to have a difficult time on their own, especially if they do not use electronics, screens, or other devices to distract themselves. Kids from difficult backgrounds and those who struggle emotionally or behaviorally are more prone to disassociate when isolated, meaning they zone out and separate from reality. However, everyone needs downtime or time for zoning out. The key is limiting this time and ensuring the child is still grounded in reality and family time.

Family projects, games, chores, sensory time, reading, journaling, and exercise or movement time are all great things to be added to the schedule as well.

By including each of these elements in your schedule, you will be able to manage a consistent routine, take charge of the day, and establish structure and safety in your home. You can download a schedule template with a list of suggested items from my website at www.healthyfoundations.com/book-resources.

CASE STUDY: LUCAS

Lucas was one of the most aggressive, angry, and explosive young men I have worked with. He was adopted at age two by a single mother who had never been a parent before his adoption. He was a strong, athletic fourteen-year-old who had physically attacked his mother on several occasions. When his mother took my parenting class, he had two counts of battery charges for assaulting her. Not only had he experienced hospitalization, partial hospitalization, counseling, and detention, but he also had a probation officer and a court-ordered mentor from the diversion program in which he was required to participate. Despite safety issues in the home, he stayed in the house under his mother's care.

My parenting course, The Family Program, was mandated as part of his probation and diversion program. His mother explained that prior to starting the program she often felt unable to care for him. His tantrums started when he was two years old, and at fourteen, he still stomped around, threw fits, and threatened or demanded to get his way. He refused to cooperate, called her vile names, and repeatedly damaged the house or her personal items. Creating safety seemed like an impossible task to his mother; Lucas's behaviors were extremely unsafe. He needed to know that his mother would not allow him to continue using controlling, manipulative, and abusive behaviors to bully the adults around him. Establishing safety was key for him to stay at home and make any progress toward a healthy and happy life.

Because of his challenging behavior, Lucas was in talk therapy, mentoring programs, and numerous other mental health services. He was given tools to use when he needed to calm down, and he supposedly had a safety plan that directed him to go to his room when he felt himself getting upset. There, he was to breathe and use his "coping skills" to calm down. However, his mother did not have tools to use when his behavior got out of control, nor did she have a way to access the safety plan on his behalf. She also did not have a safety or crisis plan of her own. So, once he got upset, she wasn't sure what to do. Most of the time, she tried to appease him, hoping his behavior would not escalate. But Lucas only became more pushy, demanding, and violent when things did not go his way. It wasn't until I met with his mother that we developed a safety plan for her that included clear boundaries and consequences around what she would and would not allow.

Mr. Rogers once said, "Children who have learned to be comfortably dependent can become not only comfortably independent but can also become comfortable with having people depend on them. They can lean or stand and be leaned upon."

Developing a Safety Plan for Lucas

When Lucas and his mother started The Family Program with me, he resisted his mother or any adult being in charge. His mother and I worked on a plan to create safety first. The plan included the three-foot rule, a structured schedule, and using space and timing to establish limits carefully but firmly.

We established a schedule to add structure, plus worked with Lucas on taking a break or doing a Calm+5 when he was upset. One boundary was to not allow him to talk back (as that was often the start of his escalation). Instead, he had to give good responses. If Lucas was unwilling to take a break or couldn't be compliant enough to listen and do the Calm+5, or if she felt he was escalating to the point of becoming dangerous, she would call his probation officer or the police.

The first morning of the program, he refused to take his medication and stomped around the house yelling and cursing. His mother and I waited together by the doorway of his room. He yelled for us to leave him alone, along with other obscenities. We waited quietly without threatening or bribing. I instructed his mother to calmly say, "Once you take your medication, we can move forward with the day." He continued to pace around, swearing and threatening, but we did not engage in his arguing. After about fifteen minutes, he took his pills while still yelling at us. We continued standing in place while he cursed and stomped around. When he pushed past us to leave the room, we moved and let him walk by. We followed, staying about three feet from him.

He proceeded to stomp around the kitchen and yell at his mother for not having breakfast ready despite knocking it out of her hands earlier. So, I instructed his mother to say, "When you are ready to stop yelling, you can help me make it." He cursed a few more times, then said, "FINE! What do you want me to do?" She gave him instructions, and he asked if he could make the bacon.

They moved through making the meal together. It was still rough, less than agreeable, and filled with rude comments. However, it was forward movement. Lucas' mother was in charge and he was going along with it. I instructed her to stay calm, and if he name-called or pushed the limits to firmly tell him that he could not continue to help with breakfast if he did not control his words and actions. He grumbled, but he complied. This all happened in the first hour of the first day with Lucas.

As we progressed with Lucas, there were times he was highly aggressive. His mother used the safety plan several times throughout the first thirty days. She called the police or his probation officer when he was highly escalated, threatening her, or getting physically aggressive. As per the plan, she was able to hold the boundary set in place most of the time and then waited for him to settle down and sit with her. He was required to sit calmly for five minutes before the next activity or task. After many days with setbacks and aggressive behavior, he slowly began to settle into the schedule, with his mom directing the day and him responding more appropriately. He learned to sit down and work through frustrations without exploding (most of the time), and he became less anxious, agitated, and controlling.

Lucas' mother was able to regain some sense of sanity and safety in her house by primarily using the tools you've already read about: the Mountain of Escalation, the Calm+5 exercise, the three-foot rule, and a schedule. I helped her identify and establish firm boundaries and consequences to Lucas' actions, which allowed him to begin relinquishing control back to his mom. Again, this took some time to bring safety to their relationship, but the tools worked because Lucas' mom stood firm and held the line. She acted to form a connection, showed Lucas she cared, and now has a much better relationship with her son.

TAKEAWAYS

Safety is the most important stone in establishing trust, love, and connection, which must be developed to bridge the gap between the child's current state and where the parent wants them to be. Furthermore, connection is crucial for creating safety within the family as it forms the foundation for all future relationships and gives the child a sense of belonging. Without safety in the home, other positive behaviors will be difficult to establish. The following takeaways are key to establishing safety in your home:

1. Parents must show that they care through consistent boundaries, structure, and a close physical presence, reinforcing that they won't give up on the child. The three-foot rule and a clear, visual schedule are two tools that are essential to establishing a safe home environment. The Three-foot Rule is a tool to help parents maintain safety by keeping the challenging child within arm's length, allowing for timely intervention and connection. Creating a clear and visual schedule for the child reinforces safety and stability as it shows that the parent is in control and provides a structured routine for the child.

2. Barriers to creating safety include the fear of taking charge, getting angry or frustrated at the child, and losing sight of the child's actions. By utilizing tools such as the Mountain of Escalation and the self-regulation techniques provided in earlier chapters, many of these barriers can be overcome.

By implementing these tools and establishing safety as the primary focus, parents can create a supportive and nurturing environment for their child, laying the groundwork for trust, love, and connection within the family.

Next, I'll build on the concept of safety by explaining how to help your child manage their emotions. When you establish methods for calming your child you can get deeper into the root of what is triggering them. Only then can you help them work through challenging situations and develop their own mechanisms for calming themselves. I also provide some very easy to implement methods that prevent escalation that I think you'll find useful, so move on to Chapter Five and learn all about regulation.

CHAPTER 5

Regulation

Has an emotion ever caused you to feel like you lost control over your thoughts, words, and actions? If so, you were likely struggling to regulate your emotions. Regulation means feeling physically and emotionally settled even when faced with or in the aftermath of stress. It is another important stone that supports the bridge you are building. It's how we manage intense emotions. We don't often notice when someone is regulated, but we can easily see when someone has lost control, or is not regulated!

Regulation is part of the bridge that encompasses safety, which is crucial in building the arch and stability of the bridge. The Calm+5 is not only used to teach children how to get calm, but it also helps them regulate their bodies and responses. To help children connect and reason, you must have a process in place that assists them in regulating their nervous system and emotional responses. By understanding co-regulation, negative cycles of interaction, and tips to increase regulation in your home, you'll develop a process that works for your family to establish regulation in your home.

CO-REGULATION

Brain science shows that people develop their ability for emotional regulation through connections with reliable caregivers who soothe through a process called co-regulation.[1] Unfortunately, many adults did not have experiences with reliable caregivers who were able to help them work through their emotions. While learning to help your child co-regulate, you might also find areas you need to learn how to regulate. One of the benefits of the Calm+5 is that it provides a tool for parents to calm their emotions, thoughts, and bodies as they stay close and help their child do the same.

Was your child taught to manage their emotions through consistent and compassionate co-regulation? Co-regulation plays a vital role in helping children to learn self-control. In fact, Bessel van der Kolk teaches that a primary function of parents is to help children to manage their moods and emotions through repeated cycles of emotional upset, followed by relaxation after parents provide calming intervention.[2] The ability to regulate our emotions is a skill that we will need throughout our lives. In times of crisis, we must learn to manage our emotions with the support and soothing presence of those we are attached to. Children who have experienced trauma, disruptions in care, or who were never soothed as small children will struggle to learn to regulate their emotions and impulses. This struggle will impact their development in thinking, relationships, self-worth, memory, health, and their sense of meaning and purpose in life.[3] But the most significant impact is the lost ability to lower the intensity and duration of their internal distress, leading to impaired higher-brain capacity that provides emotional regulation.

> Co-regulation plays a vital role in helping children to learn self-control.

NEGATIVE CYCLE OF INTERACTIONS

Mike is twelve years old and just learned that his father will not be able to take him camping over the weekend. He screams at his mother, "I hate you!" He kicks a chair, stomps around the house, throws books off the coffee table, and calls his mother a "bitch."

His scenario is not an unusual interchange for children with challenging behaviors who have extreme emotions when faced with embarrassment, disappointment, fear, or hurt. Mike's mother used to push back, get irritated, and argue with him. She would often threaten him with statements like, "Go to your room and think about what you did. I want a full apology, or you will not play with friends later!" This would only cause his behavior to escalate further. Mike would often go to his room when told to, but his escalated behavior was evident from the destruction around his room. There were many holes in the walls, his dresser was broken from being thrown over, window blinds were broken, and posters were torn down. Sometimes, it appeared that going to his room helped him settle down, but he was really just distracting himself with his gaming device. Later, once he was out of his room, his mother would be so relieved he was no longer aggressive that she avoided pushing for reconciliation and they would move on with life until the next outburst.

Many troubled young people are prone to emotional outbursts as their frustration escalates to fury and rage. Without regulation, their disappointment also rapidly transitions to depression and despair. The interaction between Mike and his mother is a classic example of a negative cycle of interaction, which inhibits a child's ability to manage their emotions and build strong relationships.

> ## Without regulation, disappointment rapidly transitions to depression and despair.

Often, teachers and parents try to take control by regulating a child's behavior with commands, threats, and punishments, which leads to power struggles and negative cycles of interactions. As a parent, you may feel it is your duty to correct behavior. You may be at a loss as to why your approach isn't working, and you become increasingly angry as you get caught up in the emotions of the moment. This negative loop of poor interactions generates more resistance and resentment and creates more oppositional behaviors in the child.

You might not like this cycle, but your child does. A negative cycle of interaction gives your child an illusion of control on some level. They may not be conscious of it, but at some level the child knows the parent is responding to something they did. The parent's reaction becomes expected by the child and they continue to escalate each other. Rather than perpetuating the cycle of negative interaction, you must disrupt the pattern and help your child regulate their emotions. This can be done by recognizing their escalation early, responding appropriately for their level, then implementing co-regulating techniques to help them calm down.

HAVE AWARENESS OF YOUR CHILD'S EMOTIONAL STATE

A person is dysregulated when they are unable to calm down and cannot control themselves internally, externally, or both. Paying attention to where your child is on the Mountain of Escalation is a key factor in noticing when your child is becoming dysregulated and knowing what to do about it. The idea is to catch the while escalating, but before they become dysregulated. However, there will be times when you miss the signs and your child is "Over the Top" before you know it. Once they are dysregulated, take time to pay attention and listen because helping them get calm starts with you as the caregiver. Don't try to reason or talk with a child who is out of their mind, or quickly escalating. Reasoning only works when someone is calm and can access their ability to understand, think, and reflect. In other words, telling them to calm down will not help.

HAVE AWARENESS OF YOUR EMOTIONAL STATE

Dr. Bruce Perry often says, "A dysregulated adult cannot regulate a dysregulated child."[4] Your child learns regulation through your interactions, so in addition to knowing where your child's escalation level is, you must also know where you are. Helping your child to regulate involves you staying calm, showing empathy, and guiding them through the process of regulation. In doing so, you become the stable object and anchor for your child. You cannot model correct behavior if you are mirroring the angry and impulsive behavior of your child. Demonstrating calm behavior and regulating together will help build the bridge to where you want your child to be. Revisit the self-regulation section in Chapter Three if you need reminders on how to calm yourself down. Though you may feel frustrated or overwhelmed, it is through connection with you as the comforting presence and stable object that your child learns to manage emotions in the heat of the moment and develop long-term self-control.

CO-REGULATING AN ESCALATED CHILD

I wouldn't be surprised if you didn't think co-regulating with your child was possible right now. I assure you that it is! Co-regulation starts with being the stable object for your child, and your family. You being self-regulated is a key part of the bridge to successfully helping your child. Next, make sure you focus on the emotions driving the behavior rather than the behavior itself. For example, focus on what is driving the anger versus reacting to the swearing. Address the disappointment your child feels, not the outburst that results from it. The behavior is just a symptom of an emotion they don't know how to deal with.

When your child's emotional state is escalated, they are not rational and even see you as a threat. Their brain is focusing on safety, or even the need for revenge, so it's not the time to teach a lesson or dole out punishment. Refrain from making threats or telling your child to take a breath, or calm down. Instead, model the behavior you want to see from your child. Remain calm, take deep breaths, be present, listen, and empathize with your child. Then, provide clear, simple direction about what you need them to do in a warm, soothing tone of voice. This builds more connection with your child than when you react with anger. Plus, it demonstrates that you are a strong, stable force that will keep them safe and guide them through the situation.

Finally, give an appropriate amount of time for your child to work through their emotions. It takes approximately twenty minutes for the brain to calm down when highly escalated. That means you can expect at least twenty minutes before they can get calm enough to even start the Calm+5 exercise. It may seem like it's taking forever, but you must hold the belief that emotions can be calmed and that the brain has the capacity to learn new self-regulation skills throughout its lifespan.

TIPS FOR MORE CONSISTENT PEACE

Dysregulated children with repetitive behavior who don't seem to respond to correction can cause parents to feel like nothing is working. Many parents become less and less confident in knowing what to do and consider giving up. Some begin walking on eggshells and do everything they can to keep their child from having meltdowns. Still, others try to become more authoritative, increase consequences, take everything away, and feel extremely frustrated because it's still not enough. No matter what avenue you have tried, you are not alone in your frustration, guilt, and lack of hope that anything can improve your child's behavior. However, I am here to tell you that you CAN change their behavior! You can even create a loving relationship with your child that fosters care and connection.

The following tips can help lower the baseline of escalation for your child and family, allowing for a more peaceful home environment. Some, such as structure and proactive intervention will be familiar as they have been covered previously. Others will be introduced for the first time and are simple but effective tips to help keep emotions calm. I recommend you read through all of them as the repetition will help drive the information home.

STRUCTURE

Creating a predictable, responsive, and supportive environment is critical to establishing regulation. Using the schedule, calendars, meal preparation, and making lists not only creates the sense of safety and order discussed in Chapter Four, but it also helps to regulate children's emotions by organizing the family. Structure also shows that parents are in charge and creates a predictable routine. Not everyone is naturally organized or structured, but efforts to have a basic plan for the day, week, or month greatly helps alleviate stress. Routines help children know what to expect and can simplify difficult time periods of the day. The schedule and routine also help parents maintain the consistency and follow-through needed to set appropriate expectations and limits for the child. They also provide more external control, which is needed for children who struggle with impulsive behaviors and lack self-control. I will discuss structure more in-depth in the following chapter.

PROACTIVE INTERVENTION

Proactive intervention heads off problems before they become major explosions. It is noticing the patterns, staying close, clarifying routines and expectations which enhance the predictability of the situation. One of the biggest mistakes is waiting until the child becomes completely undone before intervening. Look for the signs that they are becoming dysregulated and then immediately intervene. One of the biggest cues is their inability to stop and listen. If they reach the point of no return, they cannot process language and lose control over their impulses. An alliance happens when we work on establishing safety first while training our children (and ourselves) to regulate. But we must intervene early, stay engaged without power struggles, and use words that connect and change the brain to a calmer state. By being physically closer to your child (the three-foot rule), working on how you respond, and creating structure (the schedule), you can better identify the signs that your child is struggling and help them notice sooner so that they can learn to self-regulate.

CREATE A SAFE WAY TO GET CALM

Early intervention provides a safe way for children to work through emotions and get calm. In the beginning, if the child is quick to melt down or explode and you don't have time to intervene, your focus will mainly be on creating safety. As you become more aware of where they are on the Mountain of Escalation, you will also become more aware of their emotions and other signs prior to a meltdown. This awareness will enable you to take action to guide them through their emotions before they escalate further.

For example, moving in closer when they are getting frustrated allows you to provide simple, clear directions about what they can do as they become frustrated. The option of taking a break or redirecting to a different task can help the child notice the escalation for themselves. By moving in closer, you provide safety if they start to lose control, which may lead more quickly into a Calm+5, or getting them to move to their room or another safe area for them to pace, yell, and cry if they need to. But the key is staying close (close enough to support but not threaten or put yourself in danger) and giving guidance with clear and direct interventions. Remember, the higher they are on the Mountain of Escalation, the more you need to take control and offer fewer choices with less talk. Be watchful in noticing when you can offer support and guided choices or when you need to set firm limits and safety.

CALM & PREDICTABLE RESPONSES

Those who are easily or highly dysregulated cannot access executive functioning in ways that will help them reflect and think abstractly. You will not be able to talk them into acting rationally, making good choices, or calming down through reasoning. Repetitive and rhythmic activities create a sense of calm and safety. When you are doing a Calm+5 with a child or waiting for them to get calm enough to sit with you, work on your breathing to model how to get calm. Take slow, deep breaths. Children who are over-the-top dysregulated cannot take deep breaths upon command. It is helpful to work on patterned breathing in more sane times, but during the crisis, you need to take deep breaths, practice calming your nervous system, and allow the child's mirror neurons to mimic your actions.

> Repetitive and rhythmic activities create a sense of calm and safety.

Mirror neurons are a set of neurons in the brain that "fire" when you perform an action and when you observe someone performing the same or similar action. For example, if you watch someone dancing, your brain fires the same neurons as if you were dancing yourself. Mirror neurons respond to the actions observed in others, including facial expressions and tone of voice. Defects in the mirror neurons are often present in children with autism and other disorders such as severe ADHD. They are important because they help us understand others' actions. When we observe someone laughing or crying, our mirror neurons allow us to feel what others are feeling. The brain picks up and registers the emotional signals from others. Even if children are not reading others' emotions or signals, their brain can do it for them, especially if an adult is calm and regulating their emotions. The most effective way to increase the brain activity of these mirror neurons is by performing tasks that a child can also perform when they observe it. Thus, taking slow, deep breaths activates your child's mirror neurons and gives them tools to calm down without commanding them to do so.

PATTERNED AND REPETITIVE MOVEMENT

Body movement helps redirect and retain control when a child becomes dysregulated but not quite over the top. Disrupt the escalation by saying something like, "Let's do fifteen jumping jacks." This strategy will only work if they are low enough on the Mountain of Escalation. If they cannot listen and follow your instructions, they are losing control and ramping up higher on the mountain. A quick walk or having them run while you time them can provide relief. Heavy work of carrying objects during chores, digging in the garden, raking leaves, shoveling snow, moving furniture, and vacuuming can activate the child's redirection and help calm them.

Examples of patterned and repetitive activities that can regulate the brain include:

- Dancing
- Yoga poses
- Rolling cars across the floor
- Throwing a ball back and forth in ways that allow for rhythmic and predictable sequences

Musical beats also have a powerful effect on the nervous system. Adding clapping, tapping, drumming, and stomping to the schedule several times during the day can also help keep a child more regulated throughout the day. You can also incorporate rhythm into play. Simon Says, Follow the Leader, hopscotch, skipping, and building obstacle courses are great sensory processing games. These games also help develop executive functioning skills. While you are modeling calming behaviors and engaging your child in redirection through movement, you must also be conscious of what you say and how you say it.

WHAT YOU SAY AND HOW YOU SAY IT MATTERS

Have you ever noticed your mood changing to match your child's mood once they start throwing a fit? Do your words and tone of voice change to mirror your child's? When parents match their child's energy, they let the child control their words and behaviors. Parents must take charge by doing the opposite of what the child does.

You want your child to mirror a calm and regulated demeanor. One important technique is to pay attention to the rhythm, tone, pitch, and overall sound of your voice. A lower tone combined with slow and soft speech will help regulate you and your child. Humming or singing can also provide calm for you and your child. Another way to work on tone and to become aware of facial expressions is by reading out loud as a family. Self-awareness of your tone of voice, words, and actions shows your child how to regulate and sets the stage for positive outcomes.

Another tool I utilize in the Family Program is to have parents create posters that display acceptable parent-child responses. This also creates predictable repetition and can reduce reactivity in a child if they hear a response that is predetermined. This technique often helps parents refrain from arguing and giving lectures as well. The mantra responses give clarity. When a child constantly asks why or says they don't want to do something, parents can respond with a mantra like, "Parents direct the day," or a reminder like, "Your answer is 'yes, mom.'" These mantras allow the child to feel some level of independence while reminding them that the parent is still in charge. Here is a list of mantras for you to create your own posters:

FAMILY MANTRAS

Parents	Child
Who's in charge?	Parents are in charge!
All the time or some of the time?	All the time!
Why?	To keep children safe!
Who makes the choices?	Parents make the choices!
Give me a good response.	Yes mom/dad. Or, yes ma'am/sir.
Don't ask. Parents direct the day.	This is to create absolute safety.
We will never give up on you, no matter how difficult your behaviors become.	People are more important than things.

Practicing the mantras with your family every day will make it easier to use them when needed most. Remember, once the child has reached a distressed state, you cannot talk them out of it. Sometimes you may need to give the child space while you wait quietly. Slow your movements, relax your posture, appear non-threatening, and use simple sentences and a softer tone. You are the model. Rather than making suggestions or telling the child what to do, it is more powerful to be actively involved by showing that you are also working on being regulated.

TAKEAWAYS

Having emotions is part of what makes us human. The trick, however, is to not let them control our thoughts and behaviors, which is often challenging, if not impossible, for difficult children. Most people learn how to control their emotional experiences (to some degree) as a child, through a process called regulation. However, there are many factors that can cause a child to miss out on learning this critical life-skill. In these situations, it's the parent's job to co-regulate with the child, regardless of age, to teach them the process of regulation that they missed when younger.

Regulation, which refers to the ability to manage and control our emotions, is important for maintaining a sense of calm and stability, especially in times of stress. The most effective way to teach a child how to regulate themselves is by modeling the behavior that is desired. This means you must be self-aware and able to calm yourself down first. Remember, a dysregulated adult cannot regulate a dysregulated child. Model how to get yourself calm, take deep breaths, or even demonstrate taking a break to ensure a calm situation.

The easiest way to de-escalate a person is to catch them early, before they are over the top. Keeping your child close and understanding their signs of escalation will help you implement proactive intervention. Use the mountain of escalation to notice earlier when your child is agitated. Point out the observation to your child, then use an appropriate response for their current level to help them work through the feeling. Be careful not to get into a power struggle, which could easily develop into a negative cycle of interaction. You must recognize this happening and disrupt the cycle before it goes too far. Remembering your role in a heated moment is to teach your child how to regulate their emotions, and this can help you address the feeling behind the action.

Finally, you can create a home environment that helps minimize dysregulation for the whole family by implementing tools like proactive intervention, patterned and repetitive movement, repeated mantras, and structure. I touched on a few aspects of structure earlier, such as following a well-developed schedule, but the next chapter goes deeper into how structure is another necessary stone that helps build a bridge to a happier family.

CHAPTER 6

Structure

When building a stone arched bridge, each stone relies on the others to maintain stability and safety. As the stones settle, they become locked together in compression, supporting the load of the bridge and making it stronger. Structure is another important stone that helps support and stabilize the bridge you are building.

Creating structure through routine within the home environment can help you and your household boost productivity and improve your overall well-being. Structure provides external control, helps reduce stress and anxiety, and builds skills and habits for when children become more independent. Setting up habits that provide external control and guide your child into better skills and habits is powerful. This provides tools they can carry into adulthood that reduce chaos, increase confidence, and allow greater opportunity for success.

Three key areas of an effective structure include consistent expectations, consistent rules and consequences, and scheduling the day. The schedule provides a way to include patterned, repetitive activities to help your child's brain continue to develop. These types of activities help children with impulsivity, emotional disturbances, and anxiety to re-organize and regulate their brains. They should also match the child's emotional and social age rather than their chronological age. Adding age-appropriate structure supports brain growth and development and creates safe, consistent, and healthy relationships. Bottom line: structure stabilizes the home environment. So, let's go deeper into how you can set up a well-structured home, starting with consistent expectations.

ELEMENTS OF A WELL-STRUCTURED HOME

Consistent Expectations: Can you think of a time when a problem could have been avoided simply by someone communicating expectations ahead of time? Lack of clearly communicated expectations is a common source of problems. The good news is that it's easy to fix! Consistent expectations involve setting the perimeters beforehand. Even if your child is old enough to know better, their behaviors may tell a different story. By their consistently poor judgments, interrelation skills, and emotional regulation, you can probably guess what will happen in any situation in which they should know how to behave. Maybe they frequently end up in a fight with their sibling when they wrestle, throw a fit in the store while begging for extra goodies (and yes, fourteen-year-olds still throw fits), or get mad whenever they lose at Uno. No matter what the situation is, you KNOW what is going to happen. Thus, you must take time to discuss expectations and set perimeters before each situation or event. Doing so will save you time and energy in the end.

Expectations should be as simple and concise as possible, not complicated or detailed. For example, you might say, "We are going to the store so I can buy groceries. I want you to stay by the cart or next to me. I am not buying extra things today. If we get through the store without problems, we will have time to get a treat on the way home." You may also say that if they cannot stay by you without asking for things, then it will take longer, and there will be no treat later. However, I caution you not to constantly use the treat as a bribe for good behavior. It is an incentive and must only be stated in the expectations, not continually stated throughout the trip. For instance, do not make statements like, "Oops, you better be good or no treat."

Setting expectations is like providing a safe fenced yard. There are boundaries in place to keep the yard and those in it safe, but there is still a feeling of freedom and exploration. Bribes and threats, however, are like being on a leash with you holding on while they push ahead, or you having to pull them back to stay on task. This is a fear-based, limiting system that enforces strict control and quick punishment for errors, only rewarding total compliance. In a safe yard, there is freedom of movement, but the boundaries are clearly marked. There is little to no teaching with bribes and threats as well. However, setting expectations allows for learning moments which help your child improve responses and behaviors. You may have to give reminders like, "Remember, no asking," but these should be limited. If they respond poorly to the reminders, you know they are not meeting the expectations. This is where an appropriate consequence can be utilized.

> Expectations should be as simple and concise as possible, not complicated or detailed.

Determine what you will do ahead of time if they aren't responding well. In this case, you must follow through with the consequence. You may have to leave the store, go home, and continue with your day. Don't try to negotiate and don't hold it over their head or continue giving them a hard time about their behavior. Continuing to tell them that they do not get a treat since they messed up is very harmful. Use as few words as necessary if they do not let go of the situation or continue complaining about how they did not do anything or should have gotten a treat.

For example, you could say, "Yes, that is disappointing. Next time I bet you will do better." Don't talk too much about it or try to reason with them. They are fighting against an already made agreement in which they did not hold up their end of the deal. On the other hand, if they did well in the store, but then something happened causing you not to follow through on the treat, you are shooting yourself in the foot in terms of building trust and expecting future compliance. To establish trust and change their behaviors, you must follow through on your end of the deal—both consequences and rewards!

Setting expectations is critical to how the activity or day will go with challenging children. You are helping the child transition into the activity, making the expectations clearly understood and creating security. Having a plan in place with expectations as to how they should go also puts you in charge as the leader of the family. Clearly communicating expectations is an integral part that helps stabilize the bridge and so are consistent rules and consequences.

CONSISTENT RULES AND CONSEQUENCES

You can find rules and consequences everywhere in our world—from driving to the workplace. Even walking into the store, rules and consequences create structure that keep people moving and safe. The same goes for your family. Just like expectations, rules and consequences must be determined ahead of time. Writing down the rules and consequences and stating them clearly is most effective. You must also be sure that the consequences tie in with the action. For example, they might look like, "If this behavior happens, then these are the consequences…." Writing the rules and consequences this way will create a clear connection between the action and the consequence.

> Writing down the rules and consequences and stating them clearly is most effective.

Consistency has more to do with you as a parent than the rules. To be consistent, you must follow through on the consequences every time and resist giving lots of warnings and chances, then give in because your child calmed down and said please. Consistency requires intervening early to prevent poor behavior and being firm and confident in what you say. To do this, you and your child must know what actions you will take in certain situations. Write them down. Make them an agreement. Focus on priority behaviors, not every single misbehavior.

You and your family are working on a pattern of listening and doing, cause and effect, and action and response. Having actions and responses written out will help you talk less and act more when misbehavior is happening. A tantrum may follow, but it will still take less time than the process of wearing you down that often ends in both the parent and child in a tantrum. Some examples of what you could write down and post where it can be seen are:

IF THIS:	THEN:
Treating equipment, toys, or electronics roughly…	You will immediately be done for the day with that activity. We will try again later.
Don't have homework during homework time…	Time will be spent reading, journaling, or drawing instead.
Being rude, giving poor responses, or refusals…	We will wait for you or remove you from the situation to do a reset or calm down.
Getting frustrated and angry…	We will help you notice your emotion, take a break, and then try again. You can also ask for a break and then try again.
Don't put your things away…	Mom or dad will take them away for a while.
Make a mess or destroy something…	We will help you clean it up or fix it.
Need help or don't understand…	Ask for help so we can problem-solve together.
Lots of complaining…	Write it in the complaint journal. All complaints must be in writing.

Make sure the rules and consequences are clearly understood. If a rule is broken, the action on the parent side needs to be immediate and handled quickly, so that the parent can help the child to move toward the desired behavior quickly. For example, if the child gets restless and is distracting during the family reading time and is bothering his brother, the parent might usually deal with this by pointing it out, telling the child to stop, or taking something away from the child. However, it can be even more effective to pause from reading, have the parent move next to the child who is restless, pull him in closer, and then continue to read. It can help to say, "We have ten more minutes of reading, think you can make it? If not, we can end early and get started on family chore time." Remember, the goal is to keep moving in the direction you want to go. If he becomes too distracting, it may mean that you must stop reading for now, and get everyone moving into a task, keeping the child who was struggling the closest to you. You might be tempted to add a consequence and do a chore or something less fun than family reading, however, it is often best to stick with what is next on the schedule. Combining this with setting expectations helps you to be clear, consistent, and remain kind and responsive rather than harsh and reactionary. We want children to learn important concepts and skills as they grow up. These practices are less about the rules and more about cause and effect, problem-solving, and working through difficulties. Rules and consequences are also not about punishment. Rather, they are about teaching, solving, overcoming problems and mistakes, and learning as a family how to move on, repair relationships, and turn things around.

SCHEDULING THE DAY

Scheduling the day, directing, leading, and guiding allows children to relax because they feel safer with an adult in charge. Furthermore, the schedule and added structure helps to minimize arguments and family stress while improving behaviors. It puts parents in charge, which lowers the anxiety from trying to control everything. It also prevents your difficult child from being singled out since the schedule and routines apply to the whole family, which builds a foundation for success and self-confidence.

You may encounter professionals, friends, or well-meaning associates that act as if you are controlling and tell you to reduce the heavy structure for your child. They assume your children are overwhelmed with everything you have them doing to achieve better behavior, but I would emphatically say this is not my experience. Most families I work with have children who are trying to manage their environment by controlling everyone around them. And most of these children are highly anxious and need external control (structure) to help them manage symptoms. A consistent, predictable schedule provides this structure.

WHAT TO INCLUDE IN THE SCHEDULE

When creating a daily schedule, start with wake-up time, bedtime, meals, and snacks. Then brainstorm easy morning and evening routines that are manageable. Make room in the schedule for coming home from school or work and establish it as routine, so it becomes part of everyday life. Creating tasks and activities in thirty-minute increments keeps things moving and manageable. Children finish activities like homework, chores, or play in thirty minutes more often than when given unlimited time. The schedule should also include time for play, sensory activities, movement, family games, and downtime while under supervision. Feed your family at regular intervals, giving opportunity for food about every two or three hours. Snack time should be light and healthy and include a reminder that they can eat more in a couple of hours when the next meal is scheduled. Below is a sample schedule you can use for ideas to create your own. You can also download a blank template from www.healthyfoundations.com/book-resources.

Family Daily Schedule - Example

Time	Detail	Notes
7:00	Wake up (3 things to do to get ready)	
7:30	Breakfast	
8:00	Clean up / chores	
8:30	Activity	
9:00	Reading	
9:30	Learning time	
10:00	Snack & check-in / talk / connecting	
10:30	Exercise / sensory	
11:00	Game time	
11:30	Prep for lunch	
12:00	Lunch	
12:30	Clean up	
1:00	Downtime / nap	
1:30		
2:00	Exercise / activity	
2:30	Projects	
3:00	Snack - reconnecting time	
3:30	Downtime	
4:00	Sensory activity	
4:30	Journal / art	
5:00	Dinner prep	
5:30	Dinner	
6:00	Clean up	
6:30	Family time / activity	
7:00		
7:30	Get ready for bed	
8:00	Snack / family reading	
8:30	Bedroom	
9:00	Lights out	

HELPFUL TIPS FOR MANAGING THE SCHEDULE

Provide very limited choices, if any, since you and your children are learning that adults are in charge of the schedule and direct the day. Many children with sensory processing issues, ADHD, and executive functioning deficits struggle with anxiety during transitions from one activity to the next. When you give choices or leave options open for them to decide what they want to do, eat, or wear or whether they want to help, the child becomes more oppositional and less likely to comply with your directions. Choices are like transitions that build anxiety. Being specific and direct is helpful. For example, you might say, "We are going to clean up the kitchen. Tom, you put the silverware away, and Sally, you can wipe the table while I put the dishes away." This is also a good way to give them an extra sense of security by assuring them that they're not alone and you're working together to achieve the task.

Many children with sensory processing issues, ADHD, and executive functioning deficits struggle with anxiety during transitions from one activity to the next.

While moving through the schedule each day, focus on emotional regulation and relationship building rather than how much you get done. Be flexible with the structure where you can, adjusting as needed. Write changes into the schedule accordingly. Other ideas (which the child may have) can be written off to the side or on another paper to be considered another day.

Create lists of the types of things you can do, including games, tasks, chores, and meals. Remember that transitions are difficult for children, so if you try to figure out what to do in the moment, your child may feel anxiety from the unclear transition. Ensure the schedule is visible, but that you remain in control of it. Remember, you direct the day. Children need to see that the adults know what is going on. Chores and tasks are done together as a family. The child struggling the most should be your partner as you move through the activity or task.

Remember that you are helping your child cope with the chaos inside their brain and body. Surrounding them with a predictable, calm, and structured environment helps them lower the chaos in their mind. Doing this may be difficult for you, especially if you have lived with chaos up to this point, or find your own brain is a bit disorganized. The routines and structure will help you too. Many positive changes will come from following these practices, such as developing healthier habits, dealing with clutter, and distractions becoming less of an issue. These changes happen as you begin to build routines, anticipate problems, and minimize those problem situations.

Chores

Did you enjoy doing chores as a child? Most people don't prefer them. But your child will get more motivated by making them into a family activity. If your child is not participating, have them next to you as you do the task. You may have to determine an appropriate consequence for not helping with the chore—just make sure it's clearly communicated. They will start to participate over time. Also, breaking the chore into smaller tasks helps not overwhelm the child. Simply telling them to clean their room is too much. You need to go into their room and help them. Assigning specific tasks while assisting them in their room might sound like, "John, you pick up all the dirty clothes, and I will make the bed." Many children get overwhelmed with all there is to do. For example, raking a yard of leaves is overwhelming, but saying, "You will rake five bags of leaves, and so will I." is more structured and achievable in their minds.

Using a timer can also help. Saying, "We are going to clean the living room for ten minutes. Let's see how much we can get done," is more fun than pointing at the mess and telling them to clean it up. Another benefit of doing chores with your child is that it will take less time because you won't be fighting with them to get it done or continue having to remind them, only for them to get it halfway done.

Typically, chores are something adults want done, but children might not care. Pairing non-preferred activities with preferred ones will help encourage their participation. Break the chores into simple tasks using a "first and then" approach. For example, "First, we will clean the bathroom together, then we will have time to play a game." Also, remember that unless you are teaching your child how to do a task, let them do it with as few prompts or re-dos as possible. Your child will have a power struggle and less motivation if you stand over them, point out what they did wrong or what else they need to do, and then send them back to clean again. Save your constructive criticism for teaching times. Getting the task done with a good attitude and spirit of working together makes chores more enjoyable and easier in the long run. You may have to touch up the work they've done, but don't nag or tell them they did it wrong. Too much negative association will cause them to lose motivation to do chores altogether. Be thankful for their efforts and move on.

TAKEAWAYS

As you build structure and routine into your daily living, keep in mind that safety is a top priority. If the child or other family members feel unsafe in the home, structure is necessary to establish security. You are deconstructing and rebuilding the existing system that is not working well to replace it with a system proven to work. Set the schedule and tasks with lots of repetition, practice, and clear direction.

Setting up structure and routine is an investment for long-term gain. Instead of thinking, "How can I get my child to change?" it is better to ask, "How can I create a stable foundation for my child?" The structure must be stronger than their disabilities. You must think about the reconstructing process as providing a secure footing that will uphold the structure you are building. Next, I will discuss how connection will further strengthen the stones you've learned so far.

CHAPTER 7

Connection

David writes in Psalms 68:6, "God sets the lonely in families." He means that God comforts those who are alone, or lacking support by providing them a family. This also speaks to the innate and even spiritual necessity of family and community, connection, and relationships. However, there is great difficulty in families when there are severe emotional and behavioral challenges. Many times, because of the challenges, parents feel lonely, isolated, or judged by others. When there are difficulties that hinder the relationship between parent and child, parents may struggle with lack of connection with their child. Some people think parenting, raising children, and living in safe and secure families should come naturally. They think parenting skills and connecting with your child should not have to be taught because it is innate within you, and you should know how to do it without help. But parenting children with emotional or behavior challenges, and building healthy families despite a history of emotional and mental health issues, requires new ways of relating and interacting.

Building a healthy family requires parents to help their children regulate their emotions rather than focusing on stopping bad behaviors. It usually means learning to regulate your own emotions and connect with your kids even when it is difficult. As challenging as this can be, families are still best led by the parents.

Our society depends too much on services provided by doctors and therapists to replace strong parental guidance. These services should exist to guide you, not replace you. You are meant to lead your children, which is also crucial for proper child development. However, society has become child-focused, where the child makes decisions without proper guidance from the parents. Instead, we should be *child-focused* in that we should care deeply about raising healthy, strong, and well-functioning children through appropriate and effective parental guidance and connection. Creating connection is part of building a strong foundation of the bridge for your family. In this chapter, I will share methods to provide guidance to your kids while still building a connection. This includes communicating using positive responses, connecting words, avoiding power struggles, limiting choices, directing the day, and staying close while offering early support. Let's start by taking a look at communicating using positive responses.

We should be *child-focused* in that we should care deeply about raising healthy, strong, and well-functioning children through appropriate and effective parental guidance and connection.

COMMUNICATE USING POSITIVE RESPONSES

Not long ago, it was the social norm for both children and adults to address one another respectfully. For example, children were expected to address adults as Mr., Mrs., or Ms. It was common to respond to someone with respect by saying, "Yes, sir." or "No, ma'am." without it being considered militant or harsh. The interesting thing is, these polite responses are biologically better for our brains regardless of modern opinions. Ignoring, shrugging, or giving negative responses such as, "I don't want to," "I don't know," or, "I don't care" prevent the brain from producing the complex neurotransmitters serotonin and dopamine. Serotonin contributes to an overall sense of well-being and happiness, while dopamine aids in pleasure and reward[1]. So, there is actual science behind why giving a positive response is important—it improves how we feel and behave.

As previously mentioned, children with emotional and behavioral difficulties often deal with executive functioning deficits and need help building skills to increase activity in their prefrontal cortex. An effective way to help increase prefrontal cortex activity is by working on social and relational language skills. Requiring positive responses can actually help with positive thinking and actions. The areas connecting neurons get stronger with positive responses, which increases mental productivity, improves the ability to think and pay attention, and enhances problem-solving skills.[2] You might be thinking, "That is wonderful, but how do I get my child to do it?"

First, you need to create the environment for your child to give positive responses. This means working on social language cues and using words that drive connection in the relationship. Our words, tones, and behaviors are not the root of their issues, but we can communicate in a way that inspires improvement in our child. Similar to modeling regulation, parents need to set an example and demonstrate positive responses. We cannot expect our children to change if we are unwilling to change how we personally communicate. Practice positive responses every day around the house to each other. Making it commonplace will increase the chances of your child using a positive response on their own. Another way to use communication to build connection is to speak using "connecting" words or phrases.

CONNECTING AND DISCONNECTING WORDS

Rebuilding the parent-child relationship begins as the old patterns of negative, aggressive, and controlling behaviors are torn down and new patterns emerge. Building on what you've learned so far about safety and regulation, you and your child should be moving from reactive interactions to positive responses already. These simple interactions between family members are vital to the health of the relationships. Little changes in how we say something, or what we say, can have a huge impact as well. Words have the power to strengthen or weaken a connection, so changing from disconnecting to connecting words can help build more regulation, safety, and connection. The chart below lists ideas of words that create disconnection or connection between people. Don't worry if you find you have been using disconnecting words, rather note how you can improve your language to use connecting words instead.

Disconnecting Words	Connecting Words
Shame/blame words: If you had done that differently. You have yourself to blame for this. You should have…	*Observation:* Hmm, it looks like you were expecting it to turn out differently.
Shame/blame words: What were you thinking? Why are you doing that? Why did you do that? Most questions aimed at children create tension.	*Listen/Supportive:* I am going to help you with this. Let me help you and maybe you can help me understand what you were trying to accomplish. Tell me what happened from your point of view.
If you would be [nicer, study harder, etc.], this never would have happened.	Use silence and get closer, offer a hand, lean in, or lower yourself to their level.
You should think before you act. You are making it worse! You better look out! How many times do I have to tell you!?	This is hard (frustrating). Let me help and we can do it together. What could we try next time? Everyone gets frustrated, what would help?
Using punishment or fear to bring results.	Have faith in your child's ability to meet expectations that are clear and concise, even if it takes a lot of repetition.
Stop it!	Let's do _____ instead. (Redirect and give direction rather than trying to stop the behavior, unless it can be followed with action).

Disconnecting Words	Connecting Words
If you don't stop that you will be grounded (no video games/phone) for a week!	Don't use bribes or threats. Teach cause and effect. If a toy is broken or thrown, it gets taken away. Then, redirect to what they can do.
Go to your room! Get away from me!	Notice the struggle in the child and move in closer to help. Sit together if possible. Sit the child in a chair or close by for a limited time (five to ten minutes), then sit together until they calm and can move on. Do time in, Calm+5, or redirection.
Stop messing that up!	Take a time out, mom/dad!
I am done with you! Parent frustration (sigh, eye rolls, etc.).	Think in terms of how it can be resolved. Think about providing a way through the difficult situation as you redirect. What outcome do you want? The power of waiting and holding space says, "It's okay, I've got you."
Lecturing, over-explaining, answering with the "why" creates distance.	Be clear and concise about expectations from the start and don't lose sight of the goal. Move through the task or activity rather than focusing on if it was done perfectly or to your standard.

As you can see, there are many words, phrases, and even actions that we use during communication that can cause disconnection in a relationship. Strive to use connecting words and phrases and do your best to communicate from an emotionally regulated state. Continue to create safety and build trust in everything you do, which can be especially challenging if you find yourself in the middle of a power struggle.

AVOIDING POWER STRUGGLES

Have you ever had the feeling with your child that you will make them listen to you if it is the last thing you do? That is a power struggle. Children from difficult backgrounds, families with trauma, and children with oppositional behavior problems tend to get into power struggles in all of their relationships. They fight for control of every situation and conversation because letting anyone else be in charge is a very scary and unpleasant idea. Personal power is important for kids who have been hurt, or had their sense of identity and security shaken by the choices others have made. A genuine lack of trust does not allow them to feel safe, even within themselves. However, trust is built when the parent is the stable object, operating as a calm and intentional adult who leads with confidence and kindness in the child's life.

Power struggles are like playing tug-of-war—both parties pulling to win control—and kids can be amazingly strong and stubborn in this kind of battle. Even small kids willingly go toe-to-toe with full uniformed police officers. If you are focused on punishment, how they started the argument, or showing your child you've had enough, you are in a reactionary state and locked into a power struggle for sure. And you are likely being controlling rather than in control. Thus, instead of arguing, lecturing, pulling harder with a more logical explanation, or posturing to be more scary and powerful … simply let go of the rope.

Leave the argument and go back to a clear and concise directive of what is to be done in that moment. You can also quietly say, "I will wait." Move in closer while being firm, direct, and using few words. Do not start questioning (asking *why* is a surefire way to start or escalate a power struggle) or getting louder (they can hear you just fine). If possible, get on their level and be direct.

Your action should not be intimidating or about forcing them into compliance. Rather, you are applying light pressure to the situation by changing your position to be closer and more in control. If needed, an effective way to de-escalate is by making calm statements like, "It's okay. I can wait here with you until you are ready." Then, redirect them as soon as possible without bribes or punishing them. Wait for them to have the realization that it's time to calm down. Even if they huff and puff while being redirected, let it go and move forward with them. Refrain from focusing on how much you don't like their tone or attitude, or how poorly they did what you asked them to do.

> Instead of arguing, lecturing, pulling harder with a more logical explanation, or posturing to be more scary and powerful ... simply let go of the rope.

One big problem when facing an oppositional child, or someone who is challenging, defiant, or threatening, is the tendency to either overreact or disengage and underreact. Overreacting can be verbal or emotional, often producing an emotional reaction from the child as well. On the other hand, underreacting is a failure to set verbal or physical limits and can result in the adult shutting down or disengaging. Underreaction leaves the child feeling abandoned, even though they may have been pushing their parent away.

Later, when the power struggle is over, you might have an opportunity to talk through some common areas where they struggle and connect with them about the recurring problem. For example, you might say, "I noticed that whenever it's time to stop playing and get ready to leave, you seem to have a hard time. What can we do to make it easier?" Do not lecture or argue with them; simply notice if they can come up with ideas and stay connected as you brainstorm a way to manage the problem. Remember, your job is to direct them based upon the clear expectations that were previously set. If they continue to struggle with the same problem later, don't hold the conversation over their head. Avoid saying things like, "Why are you acting like this? You said you would listen when I tell you it is time to go." Instead, help them through their emotions by using connecting words like, "I can see this is still difficult for you. I'll set the timer for one minute like we agreed." This language will help them feel seen and heard while gently reminding them of the agreement.

Finally, using the mantras I taught you in Chapter Five can also help keep you out of a power struggle. These help you avoid arguments and stop parent lectures before they start. There are many instances where the mantras can be effective, as long as you use them appropriately and are not already in a power struggle. For instance, assume you are attempting to explain why you need your child to do a certain task and they continuously argue with you or complain that they don't want to do it. In this case, your responses need to stay the same. You might say several times, "Parents are in charge. I direct the day." The mantras help remind you to use short, simple, and straightforward statements without extra words. If your child doesn't use a positive response, you can gently remind them by saying, "Give me a good response." Other good mantras to use to avoid a power struggle are: "Parents are in charge," "I'm here to keep you safe," "Don't ask, I will direct the day," or "Oops, let's try again, I won't give up on you."

LIMITING CHOICES

Have you ever felt like you had to make decisions all day long for yourself, your family, and your co-workers or employees? You make decisions all day at work only to come home to more decisions about how to feed your family or handle situations with your children or spouse. By the end of the day, you feel exhausted and want to go to bed without making one more decision! If you can relate, you may understand what it's like to experience decision fatigue.

Decision fatigue can result in difficulty making good choices after being faced with too many decisions in one day. Children today are asked to make choices all day long about many things, and while kids may want to be in control, they suffer from decision fatigue easily. Well-meaning professionals often tell parents early in their parenting journey to give their children choices so they can feel in control of their day. Unfortunately, many parents take this suggestion to unhealthy levels that produce low-level anxiety in kids that is not productive for their growth and well-being. Some children do well with making choices throughout the day. Other children, especially those who struggle with behavior, need parents to direct the day, set up meals and activities, and give very limited choices. There are plenty of "lessor" decisions, like which friends to invite to their birthday party or what toy they want to take on a long car ride to grandma's house.

Benefits of Limiting Choices

Some benefits of limiting choices for your child include fostering connection and building people skills. Connection is built when what we want or are determined to have joins with the expressed will of another, requiring a reciprocal element in the relationship. Whether it is the will of a parent, teacher, or friend, relationships require give, take, and compromise. Have you ever met someone whose motto is, "It's my way or the highway?" People often act this way when they are fighting for control. Children act this way as they are learning to be relational and learn how to integrate with the wants, needs, or desires of others. A lot of people today have not learned this or have forgotten we must teach children this skill. When a child is allowed to make choices for the family about food, clothes, toys, etc., they miss out on the opportunity to learn to play nicely with others, follow directions/instructions well, or feel confident in their decision making. On the contrary, when children are given limited choices, they learn how to adapt to another person's will and work well with others, which promotes connection and reciprocal relationships.

Disadvantages of Too Many Choices

There is a strong connection between choices, anxiety, and transitions. Giving children too many choices can lead to higher levels of anxiety, which in turn creates more isolating behaviors and hinders connection. Many kids (and some adults) struggle with transitions or change. Often, transitions move from something enjoyable to something less so, which can result in feelings of dread. Giving multiple options creates uncertainty to the transition and increases anxiety further. A parent might experience this from their child as resistance, refusal, avoidance behaviors, distraction, negotiation with the choices presented, or a full-blown meltdown.

Predictable routines, schedules, using visual cues such as a timer, and clear, connecting language helps alleviate anxiety around choices and transitions. These tools also create a more positive connection with the adult or parent in charge. An example of effective transition language is, "First, we will wipe the table down, then we will have our snack." A stable, low-pressure choice is framed as, "Would you like to have fruit or cheese and crackers at snack?" If the child asks for something you did not give the choice of, you briefly repeat the choices, replying with, "Fruit or cheese and crackers?" If they escalate, or are already escalated, be clearer and more direct, such as "I will choose if you are not able to." If they cannot answer or get more upset, then choose what needs to happen next.

DIRECTING THE DAY

Having a predictable schedule puts parents in charge and helps build connection because directing the day allows you to be the leader your family needs you to be. A parent in charge builds trust, whereas a parent that isn't sure what's happening from one event to the next makes it difficult for a child to trust you. Directing the day utilizes many of the tools discussed so far such as having a visible schedule, using connecting language, giving fewer choices, calmly moving through the routines, staying as close as needed, and setting expectations at every transition until you don't need to anymore. All of these practices help you act as a stable guide, keep you from entering a power struggle, and build stronger connection. Another tool I've discussed earlier that builds connection is staying physically close to your child.

STAY CLOSE AND OFFER EARLY SUPPORT

How often could you have stopped your child's behavior by offering early support? Early intervention is a common struggle for parents. But failing to intervene early, overreacting, or underreacting drives challenging behaviors in children and leads to more power struggles and disconnection. As previously discussed, overreacting can be a verbal or emotional response that produces an emotional experience for the child. Underreacting is a failure to set verbal or physical limits, or it can be too much emotional distance from the child. When you stay close to your child, you can see and hear escalating signs before they completely unravel. When unsure, don't hesitate to move in closer or have the child come by you. Keeping your children close helps in being fair and teaching healthy interactions. Your physical presence and the power of waiting are often all you need. Don't give explanations or ask questions; simply be there in a non-threatening way. Then, if emotions escalate, you can intervene quickly and directly.

You must be consistent and firm without being intimidating. Intimidation promotes a power struggle and can cause a child to escalate and get aggressive quickly. If you are feeling, thinking, or saying, "They better do it or else! I have had enough!" or "Now you are going to get it!" you have slipped from supportive intervention to intimidation, power, control, and threats. This approach will not work. Take a step back from the situation and wait close by your child as you get yourself calm and regain your ability to interact in a clear, direct, and concise manner.

TAKEAWAYS

Strengthening the connection between you and your child are interrelated and directly correlated with building safety and trust. As your connection grows stronger, safety and trust grow stronger, and vice versa. Each of these stones are interlocked together to strengthen the bridge that will bring your family closer and heal your relationships. Focus on the way you communicate and direct the day, the words you use, avoiding power struggles, limiting choices, and intervening early while staying close. Be sure to use the mantras and polite language with your children as long as needed. Don't forget to practice getting control of your own emotions rather than trying to control your child's emotions as well. Set an example for them and they will eventually begin mirroring your behaviors.

The next chapter will continue to build on connection by explaining the value of relationships within a family. I'll discuss how we can inadvertently create neglect a child and how this impacts connection and relationships. Plus, I'll introduce the challenge that implementing changes may create for you and your child. Of course, there are always barriers to strengthening relationships and I'll discuss that too. Turn the page and add more support to your bridge by learning about the value of relationships.

CHAPTER 8

The Value of Relationships

"Relationships are the key to healing."
—**Bruce Perry, *What Happened to You?***

In his book, *What Happened to You?*, Bruce Perry stresses that healthy connections between family members are crucial for healing trauma. I would take this a step further and say healthy connections are required to heal nearly anything. It is usually within the context of relationships that people are motivated to get help and desire to grow and develop. The lack of healthy connections, as was talked about in Chapter Seven, is contributing to continued problems in our communities, families, and in individuals, and those relational problems are especially troubling for parents. You may not only see a problem in how your child is relating to those around them, but also in how you are able to connect with your child. This is because a healthy connection between parents and children with problematic behaviors is very difficult.

Many times, the relationships in homes encountering lots of challenges are strained, or barely exist at all, due to constant dysregulation by both parties, power struggles, and manipulation of love to get what each side desires. Additionally, we live in a society where quality relationships and connections are becoming weakened. There is less sense of community, less human interaction, and the norm when people are upset is to leave, or to lash out and hurt others. Add in daily demands and mental issues and life can get strenuous, especially within our families. When we feel overwhelmed or stressed, people tend to isolate and disconnect. Whether or not we recognize it, this general disconnection creates a sense of abandonment within families that affects the overall health of the family and relationships. Parents, as harsh as it seems to call it neglect, this level of disconnected inter-relational lack, must be recognized for what it is. Without identifying the disconnectedness, it will be difficult to change the way parents respond to their children and take the necessary steps to nurture healthy connections and relationships.

HOW NEGLECT AFFECTS DEVELOPMENT

Do you struggle to connect and feel bonded with your child who constantly challenges you? Are your children driving you crazy with nonstop demands, fighting, or refusing to do what they are told? Do you feel like everything with them is a power struggle where you end up yelling at each other? If any of this sounds like you, then the relationships in your family are damaged to some degree. These problems harm the family as a unit and the relationships within. The result is distancing yourself emotionally because it is just so hard to stay connected. Most people believe neglect only occurs when physical, emotional, or health needs are not met. However, neglect also occurs due to poor interactions and a relationship that is fragmented, disengaged, or includes inconsistent patterns of care. Most parents I work with have not in any way intentionally neglected their child. But many children struggle with attachment issues including lack of empathy, poor interactions with adults and peers, and are labeled as manipulative. These are signs of insecure attachment. Let's talk about how this neglect can occur.

Think about how easy it is for you and your children to all be home, in the same house (sometimes in the same room), and yet completely disengaged from one another. Many children and adults with difficult or traumatic pasts will create chaos or isolate, and sometimes they do both. Often, parents don't know what to do to bring everyone together, and more than one parent has told me it is better when everyone is in their own space and not together. However, this kind of disconnect creates emotionally hungry, needy people who long for belonging but do not have the emotional functioning or relational skills to find it. Some children are dysregulated because they are not soothed by a parent or taught how to overcome challenges with consistent, firm, and loving boundaries. Instead, parents are dismissive, or use parenting tools that create more detachment, distance, or other non-relational tactics that do not help their child to connect during hard times. Parents need tools that communicate specific, critical signals to the child's brain that are necessary for growth, empathy, and nurturing. Worse yet, the parents have no idea this kind of neglect is happening. And the child's behaviors, although linked to attention getting, are not linked to the need children have for specific and intentional parenting that will help them throughout their lives.

> Most people believe neglect only occurs when physical, emotional, or health needs are not met. However, neglect also occurs due to poor interactions and a relationship that is fragmented, disengaged, or includes inconsistent patterns of care.

Children need time and attention from their parents—especially young children. Many important aspects of development happen in the brain during the first six years of life, and having a stable and predictable caregiver is crucial during this time. A child's ability to be empathic and nurturing depends mainly on the nature, quality, and frequency of connections they experience early on in their family. One way this is missed is from early childhood trauma, which can include medical trauma. However, there may be other reasons a child misses out on normal levels of touch and interaction with a parent. Even in a biological family with seemingly normal connections and no trauma, it is possible for the child to experience fragmented caregiving. This basically means there were frequent changes in caregivers, or lack of time from parents for holding, feeding or soothing a child. It could be from moving homes, stress within the home early on, parent mental health issues or lack of consistency in routine, or how a child is soothed. The long-term effects of neglectful, indifferent caregiving or unpredictable care have proven to be toxic to a developing child. Not enough structure, even for relatively small periods of time, sends signals to the developing child that the world is unpredictable, which can lead to gaps in the child's emotional development. All of this can create chaos in the child's mind and dysregulate their emotions from a very young age. Since it starts so early, the child may just seem to be a difficult baby, or terrible toddler who quickly grows into being a challenging first grader or hard-to-manage pre-teen with a lot of mental health diagnoses.

In general, the more attentive, and loving people there are in a child's life the better. However, long-term caregivers create patterns of how they care for someone. It has been found that when a caregiver leaves, or a baby has many random caregivers, it causes emotional difficulty.[1] Parents are of course, the best and most critical caregivers for their child, however, consistent and patterned experiences with a few stable, nurturing caregivers help immensely in being able to develop healthy relationships in the future. It turns out that relational consistency is more important than we may have realized!

If you have recognized there were problems in the way you provided care early on, please don't despair, feel guilt or shame because of this. It wasn't your fault and I know you did the best you could with the knowledge you had at the time. The point I want you to understand about fragmented caregiving and how it relates to your current situation is, there are gaps in your child's development; but you can still fill in those gaps. The main idea is, there is work needed in the area of parent and child relationships, and it is never too late to make these positive changes.

CHALLENGES WITH IMPLEMENTING CHANGE

Nobody really likes to change. Moving from the familiar to the unknown is a hurdle everyone faces regardless of age or mental capacity. Even when we know the change will be better for us, it's still hard and rarely happens if we are not intentional in making the change happen. Therefore, changing how we relate, even in our closest relationships is challenging, and takes purpose. To make changes in behaviors or interactions, it is important to recognize existing patterns. Behavior patterns often run through generations of family members. Because of this, they are not always noticeable among the members. The behaviors seem "normal" and can almost be comforting because they are predictable, even if they bring results we don't like. The results we don't like, such as chaos and brokenness, is what we focus on, but we have to look at the patterns of interaction and be intentional in recognizing and building new patterns. In other words, if you want a different result in your relationships with your children and others you will have to start doing things differently. You cannot eliminate the past, but you can build new associations and new, healthier pathways in the brain that lead to healthier behavior patterns.

As you begin the process of change, children will cling to the familiar despite not getting good results. They are used to the cycle of doing the thing that causes you to react and dealing with your reaction. This pattern helps them to feel in control. They are most comfortable if you are overwhelmed and frustrated because it's familiar. But this false sense of control is not from a regulated, mindful state of being. Some of the behaviors you might hate the most could actually be the way a child has learned to self-soothe the tension inside them. These can include shutting down, dissociative behaviors (gaming and watching YouTube are examples), cutting, rage, outbursts, drugs, rocking, head-banging, self-harm, and food issues that range from hoarding to not eating. If you don't like how your child chooses to self-soothe, you must be willing to show them a different way through intentional, supportive, and present nurturing. You will need to remind them daily that they are building new pathways together with you and that the reason you are both implementing change is because they are important to you, they are loved. Remember, change is hard, and expecting the child to change without you implementing the change will not give you the results you want. Also remember, children need a lot of repetition, guidance, and structure throughout the process of change, especially when changing their subconscious programming and creating new neural pathways.

SAFETY STRENGTHENS RELATIONSHIPS

If you have ever tried to change your thinking about something, including your habits or attitude, you know how difficult it can be. This is why it doesn't work when someone demands that you stop doing something or to change your attitude. We know, however, improved relational functioning, reduces impulsive behaviors and anxiety, and promotes better problem-solving skills.[2] In other words, supportive relationships improve one's chances of success in the process of change. The relationship you build with your child is one of strength and support. Your role as a parent is to be a wise guide who knows what direction the family is going and has the patience and empathy to reach your goals together. So, you will be working on change and improving your relationship at the same time.

The first step to improving family relationships is by creating safety in your home. As discussed in Chapter Four, you create safety by setting boundaries and teaching cause-and-effect skill-building through clear expectations, co-regulation skills, good responses, and concise and clear directions. The goal for your child is for them to have a strong sense of personal worth built on self-understanding, which comes directly from primary relationships with caring adults in their life. The people they trust and where they feel like they belong depends on the acceptance, support, and security of their family and community.

POTENTIAL OBSTACLES TO BUILDING RELATIONSHIPS

Children with poor relational skills struggle with regulation, learning, and language skills. They may not respond well to instruction, feedback, or criticism. These deficits often lead to increased behavioral problems at school and in the community, which can create more obstacles for building strong relationships. Still, they need plenty of opportunities for growth, connection, and developing healthy relationships. If ostracized, even by their own actions, they miss out on necessary development. Rather than punitive and shaming reactions from the adults around them, these children need help creating strong connections and regulating their emotions before cognitive delays can be fully addressed. Thus, helping these children develop takes intentional and repetitive support from both parents and teachers.

Another potential obstacle is when relationships with children, or within families, are built around an alliance against other adults in the community. Maladaptive patterns of relationships growing up lead to difficulty in gaining and maintaining positive relationships throughout one's life. Plus, poor relationships are unhealthy for you and your child. Having an "us against the world" mentality also promotes unhealthy relationships within the home. Research shows that a community of eighty to one hundred people is considered healthy.[3] However, the health of a person or family is measured by the quality of relationships, not the quantity. Also, a healthy community does not mean it is perfect. Your goal with the school, teachers, coaches, mentors, and service providers is to be on the same team, and for your child to have the protection of the community around them. It is important for children to see the adults on the same page and not be able to play everyone against one another. Every community has its challenges. But the challenges should become opportunities for learning to regulate emotions, communicate, and repair relationships.

> Your role as a parent is to be a wise guide who knows what direction the family is going and has the patience and empathy to reach your goals together.

Your family needs interactions with other adults and other families to practice social skills. Without intentional effort to interact with others, odd, maladaptive, and impulsive behavioral patterns can lead to greater isolation and shortage of relationships. This strips the child from practicing social interaction and developing proper social skills. It is hard on children when parents bad mouth the teachers, school, counselors or other adult role models. Challenging children need to practice hard conversations, regulating emotions in public, and reconnecting and repairing relationships. They need to hear us tell stories, talk with others, and experience positive interactions with people of all ages. The fewer adult relational interactions, the less mature and more self-centered children can become. Bruce Perry teaches that relationships are the currency of change, so be intentional about creating social interactions for you and your child to practice. Who your friends are and how you interact with adults is likely to teach your child more about how to be relational (or not) than playing only with children his own age.

CREATING CONNECTION THROUGH SUPPORT AND STRUCTURE

Children who feel supported and valued experience more success. However, it is also true that many children who struggle with behavioral challenges often do not feel supported even when it is present. They will use your love and care against you, which makes it challenging to keep staying close and to keep being a solid object! When you are trying to provide help and support, there is nothing more frustrating than having a person accuse you of not caring about them. As you make these changes, they may seem small, but seemingly small challenges, or the slightest change can emotionally derail an emotionally distressed child. This does not mean they cannot learn or adjust. I find the more one struggles, the more they tend to be very detached in their ability to receive or ask for help when needed. Strength and flexibility are necessary for dealing with stress; however, your child must be taught how to be resilient when faced with big and small obstacles. They must learn to feel supported but not enabled. Each new school year, classroom, teacher, friend, and implemented change may bring challenges, but these situations are also full of opportunities to face change and build resiliency. You can help them deal with these kinds of trials by supporting them with words of encouragement and by listening before, during, and after the changes. Walk with them through the changes and challenges without dismissing their stress. What seems like no big deal to you may be a huge stress to your child. Keep in mind that their poor behavior is their way to self-soothe and communicate that things are not right. Use the tools you've learned about regulation and calm communication to model a healthy way to self-soothe and communicate when things are not right in their world.

Participation in sports, music, drama, and other activities can cause tension. However, extracurricular activities also create opportunities to help children learn to overcome obstacles. Every actor is anxious before a performance, but they learn how to work through their emotions and overcome their fears. Similarly, your child needs a way to learn how to work through anxiety and still be able to perform. If they can handle an extracurricular, this will help build their community and relationships, as well as practice overcoming obstacles. I prefer they are involved in activities within the community rather than all the days and months spent in various therapies. However, if they cannot participate, you can provide this role within the family. Remember that stress and fear shut down the thinking part of the brain, so the idea is to stay relational, supportive, and safely guide them to regulate instead of crumble.

Connection also improves regulation. When you guide your child through situations by being stable, patient, and practicing many repetitive routines and actions, their nervous system can "see" how regulation is supposed to look. Use few words, but if you must talk, stay calm and repeat back to them what they are feeling, which may be different from what they are saying. For example, "I hate baseball! I don't want to go!" might be translated as, "It sounds like you are really nervous about the game." Don't try to talk them out of what they are feeling. Let their mirror neurons match your calm demeanor while you help them work through the anxiety by being steady and stable. If you want to reward regulatory behavior, do so with connection, touch, and play rather than prizes and things. In other words, "If you get calm, you can have a new toy" is not as powerful as, "When you are calm, we can finish playing this game."

> Children who feel supported and valued experience more success.

Support looks a little different if your child behaves in unreasonable ways, lacks empathy, shuts down, is depressed, anxious, suicidal, self-harming, or acts out with anger and aggression. In that case, it's better to teach and reteach early relational skills to help them work through challenges and regulate strong emotions. Consider early interaction stages they might have missed, like good manners, communicating clearly, using positive responses, and being kind to others. They need to learn better ways to manage life so they can heal, but it will take strong, emotionally supportive parenting to bridge the gaps. Focus on connecting more and building your relationship with them as the loving leader they need you to be. Even growing pre-teens and teens need you to make eye contact, use connecting responses, sit close to them, and have quality time where you are focused on them, even if it is only fifteen minutes at bedtime. Giving plenty of hugs and playing together are also powerful ways to grow the connection between you and your child. Creating a structured environment is also crucial to providing support, regulating emotions, connecting with others, and building relationships.

Structure lays the foundation for relationships to flourish by building trust, and relationships thrive on trust. As discussed in Chapter Six, you should bring structure and predictability to daily playtime, quiet-time, and mealtime as consistently as possible. Engaging in rhythmic activities such as taking a walk, kicking a ball back and forth, shooting baskets, coloring side-by-side, dancing together, drumming, swimming, or hiking can be helpful. These sensory activities should be on the schedule but can also be used when emotions start ramping up. Remember, asking if a child wants to do something may not work as well as noticing they need to, and doing it together. Learning to stay regulated, heal, and build flexibility takes dozens of moments each day before a person can start to apply skills to these seemingly meaningless experiences. The old sayings "Weather the storm" and "Weather together" are valuable phrases to remember as you go through these changes and learning opportunities with children. Relationships that handle challenges together provide a sense of belonging and build connection.

TAKEAWAYS

Healthy relationships and strong connections play a vital role in healing trauma, building trust, and helping your child continue to develop socially. However, a child with behavioral problems makes forming a healthy relationship exponentially harder. Not impossible, just harder. One of the hardest parts is simply recognizing our own mistakes and giving grace for past neglect, fragmented caregiving, and poor interactions.

The key from this point forward is to break negative cycles and make intentional efforts to build healthier patterns in your relationships. Work on providing support, repetitive guidance, and ample social interaction for your child to develop proper social skills. Encourage participation in extracurricular activities so your child can fill in learning gaps such as problem-solving, overcoming obstacles, and having a sense of belonging in a community. Most importantly, walk through the challenges with your child to strengthen connections and create more opportunities to teach them how to properly manage their emotions and navigate challenges in their life.

Finally, if you recognize gaps in your child's development and relationships, then you are on the right path! Even if you recognize times where your relationship has been hurt, how great to have awareness in how to improve moving forward! It's worth repeating that the brain can learn new behaviors at any point in life, so it's not too late to make positive changes. Your family is going through a learning process together, and as with any learning process, mistakes are inevitable. A marker of growth is when we can take a step back, realize the mistake, and make the changes necessary to repair the error with a loving and supportive approach.

We must give ourselves grace if we want to give our children grace. In fact, this is a great goal to set for yourself, your child, and the family—everyone deserves grace when mistakes are made. The next chapter is all about setting goals and building motivation. Both are great for helping your family work through changes and inspiring hope, which means you're on the home stretch!

CHAPTER 9

Setting Goals and Building Motivation

As you move forward in building the bridge to better behaviors, it is important to consider setting goals for each child, and for the family. Most people do not learn to set proper goals, making it much harder to achieve them. Goals for challenging children should be simple, clear, visible, and achievable. When set with these elements in mind, goals can serve a great purpose in building confidence and providing motivation to your child. They are also a great way to teach accountability and keep your child (and you) on task as new habits are built.

The first half of this chapter will discuss some best practices when setting child and family goals. Then, I'll discuss how to motivate your child and improve their chances for success. Overall, the combination of goals and motivation are a key part to adding more stability to the bridge you've already started building. Plus, goals and motivation are great ways to keep focusing on the positive changes that you may not notice otherwise.

GOALS INSPIRE MUCH-NEEDED CHANGE

I understand that implementing the advice in this book is not necessarily going to be a walk in the park. I'm asking you to make major changes that impact the core of your family and, let's face it, change is always hard. Just think about the last time you had to change jobs, break a bad habit, or move.

But change is critical if you want your challenging child's behavior to improve and your family to grow closer. One thing I recommend all families do to help inspire change is to set child and family goals.

When poor behavior dominates a parent's energy and attention, goals tend to center around stopping behaviors rather than helping the child and family make real, lasting changes. If we focus solely on the behaviors, they will steal our attention away from the root of the problems and may even amplify them. Instead, the goals I encourage you to set focus on relational skills and the behaviors we want to increase. Through this positive focus, behavior will get better.

In the second week of the *Healthy Foundations Family Program*®, parents are asked to write out three goals for each child. I recommend you do this as early as possible for your child as well. As you develop these goals, keep them concise, clear and focused on small, yet positive change. Instead of writing a goal designed to stop a behavior, goals should promote the behavior you want to see. You will use them to help teach, and reteach, your child the desired skills in listening, responding, being kind, and doing what they're told. For example, the most common goals early in the program are:

- Allow adults to be in charge
- Say "yes, mom", or "yes, dad"
- Learn the mantras
- Use kind words
- Say what you need

Other skills and behaviors that you can consider when creating goals are teaching your child to give a correct response, use good tone, have kind facial expressions, show respect to others, ask for permission, accept no for an answer, apologize, ask for what they want or need, follow directions, ask for a compromise, use their words (what words and how) to express their feelings in appropriate ways, and how to recognize their own emotions.

Once you decide on the first three goals to work on, write them down on construction paper or a small poster paper. Use a separate piece of paper for each child, parent, and the family. I suggest leaving room on the paper to

Setting Goals and Building Motivation

add more goals later. Go over the goals with your child(ren) before putting them on the wall to see if there are any questions. Then, hang the papers up somewhere visible where you can go over the goals several times per day. You may run into the situation where one child is eager to make sure everyone else is following the rules. In this case, calmly remind them that parents are in charge and they should focus only on their own goals. Later, once the kids are achieving the first few goals with consistency, you can work together on setting the next goals.

I recommend that you also work together to create and write down ideas for family goals at this time. These should also be kept clear and basic, such as, "Speak kindly to one another" and "Parents are in charge." However, make sure to also add in fun goals like, "Go camping this summer," or "laugh often." Anything that increases having fun as a family would make a good goal. Kids usually come up with great ideas, so have fun with the brainstorm session. Once you have enough ideas, choose around five to put on the family goal poster and save the others for later. I've found it works really well to have a separate poster where leftover, or new ideas can be pinned as they come up. This helps kids know their ideas were heard and valued, but may not be possible yet. One family called this the "parking lot" and when there wasn't room on the family poster, the parent would say, "Good idea, go put that in the parking lot." This was a big poster board hanging up in the laundry room where mom or the kids could write down various ideas. Mom would go over the list regularly and she would add ideas from the parking lot to the weekly or monthly schedule when she could.

> ### Anything that increases having fun as a family would make a good goal.

Having goals and tracking them will help you notice small steps in the right direction that you may have otherwise missed. Any time you notice movement in the right direction, reinforce your child with encouraging comments like, "I really appreciate how much you are saying 'yes mom' today." Even on days where forward progress doesn't seem to be happening, remember to keep your responses regarding goals kind and encouraging, without lecturing. A simple but effective reminder could sound like, "Remember, we are working on saying 'yes, mom' as a good response." If the goals have been up for a few weeks and they are being ignored, or your child is struggling to manage multiple goals, focus on one goal at a time. I had one parent that did a "Yes, Mom!" boot camp to bring some fun to the effort. The girls agreed that they would do five sit-ups whenever they forgot to use a good response. So, everyone (including me since I was there that day) did five sit-ups whenever someone had to be reminded to say "yes, mom." She kept it light and fun, not punitive, so it worked quite well.

> Having goals and tracking them will help you notice small steps in the right direction that you may have otherwise missed.

Eventually, you will want your child to learn how to set their own goals, which is critical in developing tenacity and keeping motivated to get what you want out of life. Goals also provide a focus for your child and can be a great confidence booster. At the beginning of each school year, I would ask my teens to write down their goals for the year. This might include what sports they hoped to play, what activities they wanted to attend, or what grades they thought they could achieve. I wanted to teach them how to set goals and consider what it would take to achieve them. Many times, they chose goals based on their strengths and dismissed areas that were harder. For example, if they said they just wanted to pass math, or they didn't care about grades, then I would have them break the topic down a bit further. Instead of setting a goal for a specific letter grade in math, I would suggest a goal to turn in all of their math homework during the year. This was an achievable goal that would certainly help them pass math as well. Once they come up with their goals, all responsibility for meeting the goals they set was on them. It was not my job to make sure they met their goals, but I did sometimes ask, "How can I help you achieve your goals?" as part of the goal planning.

You can be supportive without taking on the responsibility of ensuring your child reaches their goals. Help them with direction if needed, but let the goal inspire and motivate your child. Setting time frames can also help motivate their efforts and prioritize tasks. I also recommend celebrating in some way when a goal is achieved. Just be careful that you are not using the celebration as a bribe, or threatening that they won't get a celebration if you don't see them working on their goal. Threats, criticism, and disappointment expressed from you will get in the way of helping kids set and achieve their goals, or be motivated to achieve them. Their primary motivation should not be to avoid pain, or to gain a reward from you, so watch out for this common mistake. Everyone experiences failure, most repeatedly when it comes to achieving goals. So, offer support and encouragement, comment on the positive changes you observe, and notice their effort consistently. These actions, along with the tips in the next section, will start to build real motivation in your child and family.

BUILDING MOTIVATION

Children are not typically interested in doing many of the tasks adults would like them to do. Add in impulse control issues and inability to accept delayed gratification, hyper focus, and their current struggles in transitioning and you have a real battle ahead of you unless you make some changes. Without intentionally building motivation, you will continue to struggle with getting your child to listen and do what you tell them. Motivating children who lack executive brain functioning skills, those with anxiety, depression, autism, or ADHD is challenging. Simple behavior charts and basic rewards and consequences fail to really motivate a challenging child. Instead, they will need structure and routines to increase motivation as well as good responses and direct, clear and concise guidance. Basically, you are going to apply many of the tools already talked about in this book. Before we get into those, however, I need you to do something that may seem impossible, but will make your life easier in the long run. While you are making these initial changes in the family, I need you to eliminate video games and electronics completely.

This is where most parents tell me their kids will completely melt down and that they won't be able to manage the child(ren) without electronics. Please trust me on this. I can tell you with certainty after all the kids I have worked with and all the homes where parents do, or do not suspend the use of electronics, this is a necessity. In order to build good motivation, they need to detox from electronics for at least thirty days. One major benefit of this is that you and your child will learn new things that interest them.

WHAT INTERESTS YOUR CHILD?

As you take charge of the schedule and eliminate time on electronics, notice the things that your child takes an interest in, enjoys, is motivated to engage with, or accomplish. Many kids doing the Family Program® discover interests outside of video games such as reading, art, family game time, sensory activities, crafts, building type projects like Legos, or even woodworking. Some kids are eager for meals, snacks, and quiet time, while others are more interested in outside activities like shooting hoops, throwing a ball around, or going for a walk or bike ride. When you have a small list of activities that your child is really excited to do, plan them into the daily schedule using the "first-then" technique.

SCHEDULE TO MOTIVATE

I'm guessing you already know what the most difficult times of the day are for your child. You may have more problems in the morning, or at bedtime. You may struggle to get your child to do their chores, or homework. No matter the task, or part of the day your child struggles with, you can improve their motivation using the daily schedule.

Put all chores and tasks that children typically don't want to do on the daily schedule. Whether they are parts of a routine, jobs, or family projects that the kids don't want to do, having them on the schedule means you can utilize the "first-then" technique. By pairing activities your child prefers with activities they don't like, you can improve their motivation to get through less desirable tasks. This is a first-then approach that works like this: First we need to clean off the table and unload the dishwasher, then we can have our snack.

> No matter the task, or part of the day your child struggles with, you can improve their motivation using the daily schedule.

Another benefit to scheduling events using the first-then approach is that it sets your child up for future success. It was taught for a long time in our society that we work first, then play. I believe this is still a great way to build motivation and resilience in our kids. There are things we must get done, in order to get to do the things we want to do. First, we have to go to work for some scheduled amount of time, then we receive a paycheck. First, we must save money for a down payment, then we can buy a house. Using the first-then technique for motivation demonstrates this concept so your child can learn this skill for the future.

Remember, challenging kids lack the skills to think first, then act. They don't fully understand that one thing happens first, then something follows. Their brain doesn't work with a mindset of cause and effect. The good news is that it's never too late to develop this concept and the best place to learn is through daily routines and structure in the home. By pairing preferred activities with non-preferred, you are requiring work first, then play, which helps build motivation, compliance, and resiliency. Of course, there may be some things that require more than the first-then technique to build your child's willingness to participate. When it comes to more challenging tasks, like chores and homework, I recommend working as a team.

SCHEDULE TOUGHER TASKS AS FAMILY TASKS

Chores are part of being in a family, but when you think about it, who is it that really cares about the chore? Often, it is what the parent wants done, even if it involves the child's room or their things. I have met a few kids that do care about things being tidy, organized, and enjoy having a clean room. This can be very helpful, but in most of the families I work with this is not the case. There are almost as many arguments and power struggles over chores and cleaning up as there are about homework or getting ready in the morning.

Put chores, homework, and other tasks where you receive the most resistance on the daily schedule using the first-then technique. Additionally, set it up so everyone does chores together. Pair up with the child that is the most resistant so you can be close and provide guidance if needed. You aren't there to force them to do the chore as this often leads to a power struggle. Instead, simply keep your child close and encourage them to work with you. Most kids will start to help if you and other siblings are working at the same time, and if you have a "let's get this done together" attitude.

If you have several kids then you can work together on a larger project like cleaning the kitchen, or organizing the garage. If the chore has multiple parts to it, break it down and give out simple and clear directions. For example, instead of, "Clean your room," try "Put all of your dirty clothes in the laundry room." Give them specific tasks to do and keep them busy with helping. Pair an older sibling with a younger one if they are able to get along. It is still best if you can be nearby to monitor and be a part of it with them. The bottom line is that humans have a tribe mentality and everyone wants to feel useful, whether they act like it or not. So, when everyone is pitching in and helping with a task, you are much more likely to eliminate resistance from a challenging child.

> **If the chore has multiple parts, break it down and give out simple and clear directions.**

Provide positive reinforcement if the chore takes less time than scheduled. Do not add more chores just to fill the time, as this will lower motivation. I recommend keeping the time for chores to thirty-minute blocks and make sure you are clear about what should be accomplished during the time. Also, do not make the common mistake of getting too nit-picky over details. Motivation for tasks like chores is greatly lowered when a parent primarily acts to oversee them and point out what still needs to be done, or how something wasn't done correctly. Keep in mind that the goal of chore time is participation without resistance. If you need it to be done perfectly, plan some time to go back over it later. That being said, I do think it is important to take the time to teach your child how you would like things to be done. Teaching them while working together is not the same as criticizing how they are doing something. You can also teach your child to break tasks into three smaller steps to make it feel easier.

SIMPLE IS MORE ACHIEVABLE

Having three steps can help motivate you and your children with chores and routines because each smaller task is less daunting than the entire assignment. Cleaning their room may seem overwhelming and open-ended. However, if they break it into three steps the process will seem more achievable.

An example for cleaning their room might look like the following:

- Put all the dirty clothes in the laundry room.
- Pick up all the toys on the floor.
- Make your bed.
- In the morning, try to keep what they need to do to get ready to three steps as well.
- Get out of bed and use the restroom.
- Comb hair and get dressed.
- Eat breakfast then brush your teeth.
- Another example to help with their after-school routine might look like:
- Put backpack, coat, and shoes where they go.
- Use restroom and wash up.
- Get a snack.

Again, do not add more tasks if they get done quickly. This is critical. I think a lot of kids deliberately go slow just so less is expected of them. Instead, thank them for finishing quickly and build in more incentive to encourage more of that behavior.

INCENTIVES INCREASE MOTIVATION

The last tool to build motivation is to consider adding incentives for good behavior. Can you stop for a donut on the way to school if everyone is ready fifteen minutes early? Is there time for a family outing because raking the leaves went much faster than we thought? Can you surprise the child who did an extra great job cleaning the bathroom with a huge thank you? You don't have to be over the top with it, but a little something extra that your child wasn't expecting reinforces positive behavior. One important concept to understand, however, is the difference between a bribe and an incentive.

Bribes and incentives are not the same. Bribes attempt to motivate by using the preverbal carrot on a stick. It is something you present before a task that implies they will only receive the reward if they accomplish the task the way you want. Bribes are usually arbitrary and have nothing to do with the task.

They can also be easily converted into a threat—*if you don't do this right now, you won't get any candy*. Incentives, on the other hand, are rewards based on achievement, not something held out like a carrot on a stick. This type of reward is much more logical and has been proven to build motivation. An incentive can be as simple as expressing extra gratitude, it does not have to be a physical reward. Also, keep incentives random so there is no expectation for a reward, otherwise they just turn into bribes. This is one reason I do not recommend paying your child for basic chores that are on the daily schedule. Ultimately, it is best when children learn that some things simply have to be done, and others deserve compensation. Regardless of the task, however, the goal is to build motivation and encourage positive behavior.

TAKEAWAYS

Setting goals and building motivation increases compliance and reduces resistance many parents face from challenging children. Of course, goals and motivation alone will not "fix" your family. However, utilizing the many tips in this chapter along with the tools and tips from previous chapters will build the bridge you need to become the family you envision. Have patience and give yourself grace. None of this is easy and it will take a little time for everyone to accept extra structure and settle into a new schedule. Goals are a great way to incentivize this necessary change.

When setting goals for your children and your family, start small. Make sure they are simple, clear, and achievable. At first, goals should be set to reinforce positive behavior, such as good responses and being courteous to others. Later, you can teach your children to set their own goals and determine what is needed to achieve them. This is a skill that will serve them for a lifetime and is amazing at increasing confidence and motivation.

Building motivation in your child is also essential to success in the home and in life. Self-motivation is part of executive functioning skills that are typically underdeveloped in challenging children, and can significantly impact your child's self-confidence, school performance, and outlook for the future. Build motivation by putting tasks on the daily schedule that usually draw resistance followed by activities that interest your child. The first-then technique can inspire your child to get through the hard moments in order to get to something they enjoy. Also, make chores and other events that aren't as fun a family affair. This will invoke the tribal desire to contribute from your child as they see everyone participating to accomplish a goal. Don't forget to break down complex chores into simple tasks, or three steps, in order to reduce the likelihood of getting overwhelmed. Finally, offering gratitude and incentivizing good behavior can dramatically increase motivation.

Keep in mind that the goal throughout all of this is to connect with your child and strengthen your relationship. If your child feels connected, it is much more likely they will contribute without resistance. Encourage them often to boost confidence and they will begin to feel they are capable and deserving of success, which also reduces friction.

Just like everything else I've taught so far, stay consistent and you will significantly increase your chances of success. Setbacks are to be expected, so don't assume these tools aren't working if your child still has a meltdown once in a while. Just keep using the tools and focusing on the stones you've learned and you will see improvement! I'll provide a few more tips and some answers to common questions in the next chapter, so get ready to add a few more things to your bag of tricks!

CHAPTER 10

Tips and Tools to Build a Better Bridge

As you work on building a better bridge for your family, you will inevitably encounter problems and have questions. Each family's circumstances are unique, but parents frequently experience similar issues and have common questions. The following paragraphs offer advice and answers based on common concerns. If you require additional help, I invite you to join our Healthy Foundations Family Program. The program offers tailored plans for each family based on their unique circumstances, providing the necessary tools, guidance, and support for lasting change.

My daughter is nine years old and loves to draw me into a power struggle. How do I keep from getting into arguments with her?

Avoid arguing with your child by refusing to engage. While it sounds simple, it can be difficult to resist the urge to argue with a child who insists on having the last word and controlling every situation. Remember to recognize where your child is on the mountain of escalation. Regardless of how much you want to persuade them, get in the last word, or make a good point, engaging in argumentative conversation, debating, or negotiating is an unhealthy approach. Refuse to enter an argument, even if you believe they will listen. Use simple, clear, and concise phrases, repeating them as needed. For example, if you feel your child is pushing you into an argument, hold up your hand and say, "We will talk about that later. First, you need to get calm/take a break/finish your task." If they continue pushing, repeat the phrase, saying, "We will talk later." After that, disengage and stop responding altogether. If you must say something, use minimal words and be direct. Try a short statement such as, "After you are calm." Remember, the situation is like tug-of-war, so you must let go of the rope instead of trying to win.

It seems like there is an overwhelming number of things we need to fix. Where do I start?

Pick one main skill to work on daily. Start each day by setting an expectation for your child that the skill everyone will focus on for the day is _____. For instance, as you start breakfast you can inform your child, "Today we are working on giving good responses," or "I want today to be a good day. We will work on saying *Yes, Mom,* or *Yes, Dad* when responding. I will give you some reminders, but I know you can do this without them. I hope you will work hard with me on this today." You can follow the same structure regardless of the skill you hope to improve in your family. Keep in mind that building new habits requires significant practice, so connection, patience, and empathy will be required to succeed.

My fourteen-year-old often complains, or tries negotiating to get what she wants. How can I stop the complaining?

Set a rule that all complaints must be in writing. Give your child a notebook that is only for writing down complaints and set the expectation they must be written down to be considered. Then, when a situation arises where your child starts to complain, say "I will consider that idea. Please put it in writing." If they keep complaining, do not engage. Instead, repeat that they need to put their complaint in writing. There may be times when your child has a legitimate point and you are open to doing what they want. In this situation, continue to reinforce cause and effect by granting the request after it is written down. Follow through on your promises, as failing to do so will hurt your credibility. Your child will not trust you, or continue using the notebook if their complaint is never considered, so look for ways to use positive reinforcement and show them that they can get their way sometimes if the proper procedure is followed.

What should I do when it comes to arguing about doing chores?

Throughout the process of building healthy family foundations, chores and similar "less fun" activities are part of family life and the daily schedule. All chores should be done with a parent until the child gets better at helping without resistance. If they begin to argue or complain about the chore while with you, calmly tell them that you don't want an argument (as a warning) and inform them of the consequences if they continue. For example, "I don't want to argue. Let's finish this quickly so we can move on to our next activity. If you choose to argue, I will set the timer and you will need to get this done by yourself." You can change the second phrase for other options, such as, "We will have to take a break until you are calm enough to continue." Telling a child that you will complete a task together reduces complaints, arguments, and resistance around chores. If they are unwilling to help, ensure they stay close to you and don't allow them to do anything else while you complete the task. Usually, kids will start to help because they are too bored otherwise.

I don't want to be rude or mean by bossing my kids around. Isn't it mean or militant when parents are in charge?

It is not mean or militant when parents are in charge as long as they are regulated and respectful when giving direction. When communicating with your child, it is important to be clear, concise, and direct. Do not over-explain, lecture, or resort to yelling. You can calmly and firmly tell your child what needs to be done, such as, "Your job is to do the dishes. Please do that now." Then set the timer and say, "The job needs to be done before the timer goes off." You can model being polite while still being clear and direct. Parents who are not used to speaking this way might feel awkward or unnatural at first. However, you must continue to practice speaking in a calm but firm manner toward your child to build a healthy bridge and be a stable role model. Your child might say things that make you feel guilty for the new rules you are establishing, but you must stand firm and confident in knowing you are in charge and doing what is best for your family.

What if my child doesn't complete a task on time?

If your child fails to complete a chore on time, tell them the time for that chore is up and it's time to move on. The consequence for not getting a task done needs to be decided ahead of time. For example, you can inform them before they begin the chore, "If you don't get the dishes done during chore time, then we will have to finish them during game time." Ensure the fun activity being replaced with finishing the chore is close to the time that chore was scheduled. Replacing the activity with the chore will not work if it is more than an hour or two after the chore. Choose a fun activity as close as possible so the child can make the connection. When chore-time is up and they have not finished the task, you might say, "Oh, I see you did not get the job done. Chore time is up and we are supposed to have playtime now, but you will need to stay here with me while I finish up." If you can finish the chore together, the child can have the remainder of the time for the activity. Decide ahead of time what will happen if the chore is still not done. The consequence should be uncomfortable for them if they choose unwisely, but do not punish them with more chores or force them to complete the task.

I can't take my kids to the store because they always misbehave. What do I do?

Before engaging in activities that have caused difficulties in the past, establish clear expectations in advance. Inform your children what you will do during the activity, what their responsibilities are, and the consequences if they don't follow the rules. For instance, "We are going to the store and I need to get all the items on this list. While we are in the store, I want you to stay by the cart without asking for extra things. If we have a successful trip without problems, we can get home in time to play a game. If we have a problem, I will only give one warning. After that, we will leave and not have time to play at home." Having them repeat what they heard ensures they understand your directions. Give a gentle reminder about what you want them to do before you leave the car, for example, "Remember, let's get this done quickly and stay close to the cart." Don't dwell on the things they did wrong in the past. Instead, stay focused on the expectations and maintain a positive attitude. When they perform well, encourage them by acknowledging their effort and perhaps surprise them with an occasional treat as an incentive. Be careful not to go overboard with incentives as children tend to meet our expectations. The goal is for appropriate behavior while shopping to be a normal occurrence that doesn't require constant rewards.

What should I do when a child breaks a rule and fights about the consequences?

Setting expectations in advance is crucial. Be sure they know the rules and what happens if they are broken. Before starting a game, make sure the rules and consequences are clear. For example, "During the game, if a piece in your pile falls on the ground, you will lose it, and it will go in the middle of the game. Is that clear?" If the child violates the rule, gently remind them, "That piece needs to go in the middle." If they argue and complain, gently reiterate, "I told you the rule beforehand. That is the rule, and you must follow it. The piece goes there." The child might continue to complain. In that case, you may have to wait until they calm down before you can continue. If they get more escalated and continue arguing, tell them, "I am sorry, but the game is done since you don't want to play by the rules." Then you can put the game away. Children who argue their way out of everything need to have a very small world where they keep bumping into fences (expectations) until they learn to respect the boundaries and play in the middle. Being consistent, staying calm, and following through with expectations and consequences is important.

Shouldn't there be more consequences when they break the rules?

Children need to learn through cause-and-effect parenting. It is best to keep things simple and tie the consequence to specific action that occurred. This way, we teach kids that the actions they choose have corresponding consequences they do not get to choose. As a parent, this allows you to follow through on the consequences without being swayed by their charm or arguments. Writing down common actions and consequences on a chart helps them to make the connection. You can begin each phrase with, "If this happens, then this …" Keep it simple, such as, "You were not safe, so now we must sit and get calm." Do not ground or punish the child for a length of time. Implementing consequences in the moment is more effective than any punishment carried over time.

When my child wants something, he whines and sometimes screams until I give it to him. If I say no, he becomes very upset! I know giving in to his demands is not good, but what can I do?

Initially, your child may need to learn to give good responses and accept your guidance as the parent. Children with behavior challenges often want to do things their way and according to their schedule. However, they must first learn to give an appropriate response before being allowed to make a proper request. During this learning process, they must also learn to handle the disappointment of being told no, or not yet. It is beneficial to teach toddlers this lesson as early as possible. When a child has a meltdown due to not getting their way, you must help them calm down while standing firm in your decision to not give them what they want. This way, they can eventually learn to overcome such negative reactions. Even if your child is a teenager, they still need to be taught how to accept disappointment and not get what they want by throwing a tantrum.

How can children learn to accept no as an answer, or make requests appropriately?

Children need to learn that bad behavior will not get them what they want. Teach your child how to make a proper request to prevent whining, arguing, and yelling. Do not accept that behavior when your child wants something. Teach them that if they do not make a request properly, the answer is going to be no and arguing will not change anything. Instead of giving in, parents should respond with statements such as, "Oops, try again without whining," or "Please try again using kind words," or "I understand you want it, but you will need to wait."

Parents should not react, but instruct their child by telling them exactly what to say or giving one of the above responses. Some children also react nonverbally, refusing to use words or full sentences. If a child does not want to do an activity and refuses to join you at the table, they are not making their request properly. Teach them to communicate appropriately, such as saying, "I don't want to play that game. Can we play a different one?" Parents can honor the child's ability to communicate properly and suggest other options. However, if they reject every suggestion, it is still not an appropriate response to parents directing the day. In this case, parents should cancel the activity altogether.

Can you provide examples of how to set expectations?

You must set expectations before starting any activity! This includes explaining the plan and what will happen if things do not go well. The following examples illustrate how to set expectations properly:

Example 1: "We are going to have a snack, and the choices are on the table. Please don't ask for anything else because the answer will be no. You don't have to eat if you don't want any of these choices. However, I expect you to sit with us at the table during snack time."

Example 2: "We are going to play this family game. Someone will lose and someone will win and that's okay; there is no prize for either. During the game, we are focusing on how we treat others and encourage one another. When the game is over, we will put it away and congratulate the winner. If you get frustrated or upset during the game, we will wait for you to calm down, then continue playing. However, if you cannot handle it, we may need to pause the game while you take a break or stop playing altogether. Okay? Let's make sure we know the rules …"

Why is it so difficult to change their behaviors? Why can't I simply make them stop?

Change is hard for everyone. The brain is complex, and our behaviors are often the result of a combination of factors, such as genetics, upbringing, environment, and personal experiences. Even as adults, when we want to change or break bad habits, we can become stressed, depressed, and anxious. When it comes to our children, we often fail to realize how even small changes add up over time. Usually, kids don't want to change because their behaviors serve them in some way. They are not always conscious of what they are doing and don't fully understand how it affects them or the people around them. This is why you must initiate the changes.

If you want to change your child's behavior, you must change the way you interact with them. Disrupt the cycle of negative interactions and change the dynamics of what is happening within the home from the top down. It may seem futile to make a schedule, direct the day, or do chores and tasks with them. And requiring them to say "Yes, Mom and Dad" may seem silly, or too demanding. However, all these rules and expectations will change the dynamic within the family relationships and ultimately transform behaviors. You will be amazed at the results if you exercise patience, persistence, and use the right tools and techniques.

A FINAL NOTE

Keep in mind the kind of relationships you want to have with your children. As they learn to listen and follow directions, they experience less anxiety and more joy in life. Chaos is reduced and families become capable of doing more things together. Remember, repetition is key for both you and your children. Don't give up! In the Healthy Foundations Family Program, I work with families to restore hope and bring their vision of what their family can be to life. You are not alone in this journey! Many other parents are working on the same changes to build stronger families with kind, resilient children. I highly recommend you join a community of parents going through similar challenges where you can ask questions, share stories, and enjoy much-needed support. My private Facebook group for those who have done my program and readers of this book, www.facebook.com/groups/ 2608939022734486, provides just such a community and I would love to see you in the group!

CHAPTER 11

Bridge to Change and Future

What images come to mind when you think of a healthy family? You may picture people who encourage open communication and loving conversations. Perhaps you envision family game nights, or evening walks full of laughter and fun. Support and encouragement during personal challenges might also come to mind, such as a child's new after-school activity or a parent's career change. Whatever you visualize likely seems distant from your current family situation. However, reaching your goals is entirely possible, no matter how far away they seem. Certainly, embarking on the journey toward a healthy family environment can be both challenging and rewarding. The most powerful approach when starting your journey is to make small, yet significant changes that will create a lasting foundation of love, understanding, and connectedness. The following parable, written by Jo Wenger, is a great representation of the work you are about to begin.

THE PARABLE OF THE COBBLESTONE BRIDGE

A bent-over, elderly man rested the weight of his body on his cane. He gazed over the swirling waters raging under the most amazing cobblestone bridge he had ever seen. It wasn't that it was particularly beautiful—the rocks didn't necessarily fit perfectly together—but he was one of the few people that was privy to the amazing story behind the bridge.

It all started when a young man, so many years ago, was standing on one side of the raging waters. The man was full of despair and hopelessness as life had not turned out as he had planned. In fact, he still couldn't understand how something which was intended for so much joy and fulfillment felt so much like a prison to him. "Is there something wrong with me?" he asked himself often.

One day, an old man saw the slumped shoulders of the young man and paused to inquire about the reason behind the depressing posture. The young man wistfully gazed over the waters and pointed to the beautiful scene beyond the river. He mentioned that the peace and beauty of the open grass with flowers and trees on the hills beckoned to him. He just knew this was the solution to his problems, but there was no easy way to get there.

The old man, to the surprise of the younger man, agreed with him. And not only that, he promised that he was a guide to help people get to their destination. Although the young man was skeptical, he turned to question the old man about how that could be possible.

The guide explained that it was actually quite simple. Not easy—but simple. He said that he will teach the young man how to lay a strong stone foundation as a base for a bridge. But it was up to the young man to add to it. "But how?" inquired the young man, "I have no skills, or experience." The guide offered, "It takes no specific skill to start, just a willing heart and some hard work." "How long will this take?" asked the man. "It depends." stated the guide. "Some people do it quickly. Others take years. Both are totally okay. It's not a race." The young man, now full of hope and determination, asked "How soon can we start?"

And so the journey began. The wise old guide worked with the young man stone by stone to lay a strong and secure foundation for the bridge. When that was done the guide explained the next steps, then stood up, wiped his hands on his pants, and said, "The rest is up to you."

The young man was astounded, confused, and not at all confident in moving forward. But the guide assured him that all he needed to do was take the very things he had just learned and do them over and over with smaller stones and he would be successful.

The young man was still skeptical, but looked longingly to the other side and went to work immediately. Some days, he rejoiced because he was able to place lots of small stones on the bridge. Other days, he was happy to just get one placed. Sometimes he dropped the stones in the water in his attempt to hurriedly complete the bridge. And then some days he couldn't manage to get a single stone placed no matter how many times he tried. But, on the days that he felt especially discouraged, he thought back to the beginning and realized how much progress he had made, and he felt encouraged again.

Eventually, the day came when the young man was able to walk the whole way across the bridge. He could hardly contain his excitement at the possibility. But to his dismay, once he crossed the bridge, he realized all of his problems followed him. He sat down in the grass on the other side of the bridge with his head in his hands.

At that moment, his guide mysteriously appeared once again beside him and inquired of the depressed posture of the young man. As the young man explained his disappointment that nothing had changed and still felt like the same prison, the guide helped him to his feet. "Look around you," the guide said "and tell me what you see."

"Oh!" the young man slowly exclaimed. "It is different! Why is it that the problems around me look so much smaller and easier to manage? And why does that give me so much peace?" The young man was truly puzzled.

"The secret is the bridge." the guide answered. "Look at the thousands of stones you placed. You took what I taught you and practiced it over and over and over again until it became natural and easier. You changed in the process and you didn't even notice. But I did. I watched you from a distance each day with a smile on my face, knowing that your future is forever changed due to your commitment and willingness to do the hard work, through success and through failure. And the bridge still got built, so embrace your future. And although you have no idea how this bridge has changed you, I know that it has changed more than you. The impact will be felt for generations to come. Well done, young man.

The bent-over old man adjusted his cane and smiled to himself, then walked away. Although his guide never appeared to him after that last amazing day, he often wished for the opportunity to tell him how he has already lived long enough to enjoy seeing his family thrive—all because of what he learned in building his beautiful cobblestone bridge.

The power of big change comes from lots of small, consistent, and meaningful efforts. I love the similarity between Jo's parable and the work you are about to embark on because it represents the journey and effort needed to cross the turbulent waters into the peace and joy you desire.

The larger stones that secure a strong foundation for the bridge are safety, structure, and relationship. Establishing these are required to be able to build upon the foundation and continue to expand from the base level. Without these foundation stones in place, the smaller efforts will simply wash away in the turbulent waters and your bridge will not develop. However, with these in place, your daily efforts to direct the day, teach good responses, model emotional regulation, stay close and create connection, and fill gaps where brain development missed opportunities will act as the small stones, dirt, and mortar that will continue to expand your bridge to reach the other side. Just as the parable states, there will be days when the small rocks fall in the water, or you can't seem to get it right, but that doesn't mean what you are doing isn't working. Stay consistent with small changes and you will soon be able to cross the bridge to the other side.

SMALL CHANGES EQUAL BIG RESULTS

Think about what changes you want to see and what kind of family you want. Strangely enough, I would encourage you to think small. Not small in the overall transformation you want for your family or your child, but how small changes can have a major impact on the behavior of everyone involved. Illustrating the point about how important small changes can be, and why they should not be overlooked, is the Broken Window Theory.

The Broken Window Theory

Imagine a city with trash and graffiti throughout the streets. Old, beat-up houses fill the neighborhoods, some of them abandoned with broken or boarded-up windows. Even the stores and gas stations look run-down and dirty. Would you consider this city a place of order and safety? Probably not. The reason for this can be explained by The Broken Window Theory.

Developed by social scientists in 1982, and made popular by Mayor Rudy Giuliani and the New York City Police Commissioner in the 1990s, the theory proposes that crime is the inevitable result of disorder. For example, if a broken window remains unrepaired, people will conclude that no one is in charge or concerned that the wrongdoing occurred. This leads to an attitude that anything goes, similar to the lawless Wild West. The theory prompted some police departments to establish training, guidelines, and supervision for developing positive relationships in communities.[1] The mayor of New York understood the power of small modifications when combined with this theory and used it to begin implementing positive changes throughout the city. He started by cleaning graffiti off the subways and quickly repaired each car, one by one. It was a small expression that put the broken window theory into practice. The mayor and police commissioner swiftly dealt with smaller issues, like following through on expectations that the system was sustainable and those doing wrong would be held accountable. These small efforts led to big improvements in the crime rate and made New York City safer.

The Broken Window Theory also applies to family dynamics, as leaving things broken and unrepaired creates a sense of carelessness, chaos, and lawlessness in the home. The theory emphasizes the need to establish a stable, predictable, and orderly environment to prevent further behavior problems. In The Healthy Foundations Family Program®, families dealing with high levels of aggression and destruction in their homes see significant changes when they deal with smaller issues first. A high level of chaos in the home symbolizes a collapsed system. Thus, first addressing the smaller issues, such as scheduling, establishing routines, expecting good responses, and maintaining a clean and organized home, makes a big difference in restoring a sense of order and control. Children, even those who seem to be living in their own world, are very sensitive to their environment and attentive to cues around them. Small actions and intentional, early interventions throughout their daily routines matter.

Parents play a vital role as leaders of the family unit. If no adult is in charge, those responsible for wrongdoing are less likely to be held accountable. Since wrongdoing is contagious, poor leadership only leads to more disorder. By creating an environment that shows children that their actions have consequences, parents foster a sense of security and connectedness within the family. Intentional parenting and careful implementation of structure and connection that is based in safety and healthy interactions are a vital part of implementing change. Focus on consistent, small efforts throughout the day and watch how fast they add up to big results. A common mistake I caution you to be aware of is getting so caught up in the process that you fail to recognize improvement.

RECOGNIZING IMPROVEMENT

You may remember the exact moment when you realized you were not in control, or that your family was not normal, and feel like things changed overnight. However, I assure you that "moment" developed slowly. In other words, it was only your realization that you no longer had control that appeared to happen quickly. The change that brought you to that point occurred moment by moment, every day, over the course of years. The same concept is true when reversing the behaviors and chaos that currently run your family. It will take thousands of small efforts, day after day, to reach the desired outcome.

Parents are often the last to notice when a child has made improvement and the family environment is changing. One reason for this is that parents tend to be skeptical and may not believe the progress is real, so they unconsciously filter it out. Another is that it's hard to notice change when it occurs over a longer stretch of time. Incremental progress can be adapted as normal behavior before you are able to recognize and classify the change as improvement, so it goes unnoticed. Or, parents fail to recognize improvement because they are looking for big, dramatic changes instead of small, incremental ones. One way to avoid these traps and see improvement earlier is by measuring your progress.

Sometimes, it takes looking back to realize there is less chaos, better responses, and increased happiness. It's not always easy to see moment by moment, so I recommend keeping a journal and tracking specific data to make progress easier to spot. By journaling at the end of each day, you will start to create a record of behavior that you can reference along the way as proof that what you are doing is working. Over time, you will see small improvements that might otherwise be overlooked.

Metrics that you may want to consider tracking are:

Rank the level of chaos for the day on a scale of one to ten. When operating in a chaotic environment, the brain has a hard time remembering details and specific moments. Days start to run together and "good" days can easily be overshadowed and forgotten by a really bad day. By ranking the chaos level each day, you create a record that serves as the baseline for your family. This data will not only prove that improvement is happening, but it will make it easier to believe it is real when you see lower average rankings after a few months.

Log how many times, and at what level, your child peaks in escalation. Similar to ranking daily chaos, this provides a baseline of escalation for your child. They may peak two to three times per day in the "Over the Top" category at first. This is important to know and will help you determine when improvement is being made. As you consistently implement the tools in this book, you may see your child reduce to one peak per day. One major escalation is enough to make you feel like no progress is being made, but looking back over your journal will help you see that change is happening and to keep up the work.

Log results for individual and family goals. After you set goals for your child and your family, it will be helpful to log results to see progress easier. Make note of a specific skill you chose to work on for the day and how it went. This can be general or specific depending on the goal, but it should be clear enough that you can compare early days to days a few months down the road. Your child should be tracking their goals themselves, but your record may be a little more accurate at reflecting reality. Any positive change noticed adds motivation and hope to a long process, so don't be afraid to track small goals that are more easily accomplished along with the bigger ones.

Write about areas where you are struggling. Nobody is going to start a process like the Healthy Family Program and execute every aspect of it perfectly and easily. You may struggle more with self-regulation and staying calm, while another parent may struggle with directing the day, or maintaining the schedule. When you write this down you can see where you need to improve, or may need extra help as well. It will also help you see your own improvement by comparing early journal entries to those down the road.

Write at least one daily victory. This is the one suggestion that I feel is so important it should not be skipped. Even if this is the only thing you log, looking for victories in your day is incredibly powerful at shifting your vision to recognize positive change. Victories can be as small or large as you need, but make sure to look at each day and find a positive moment. Then, take a little time to express gratitude that you experienced that victory. Try to make this the last thing you do with your journal so that you end the day focusing on something positive and with gratitude. You will be amazed at how much better you sleep and how your attitude is more positive in the morning.

Of course, the above list is nowhere near all-inclusive. Use the prompts above to inspire your own ideas about what's important for you to journal about. Be patient with this exercise as well. I've already discussed how change takes time, so it may not be obvious in week one that improvement is happening. However, if you trust the process and stick with the program, you will find a point where the data shows your efforts are paying off. Every small effort is significant in building something substantial and using a journal to document your journey will help you recognize the changes as they occur and realize milestones of success.

WHAT DETERMINES SUCCESS?

You get to define the standards you want for your family, so set goals and make them measurable so you know when they have been met. Celebrate milestones as you reach them to keep encouraging progress and inspiring hope within your family. You may even consider a milestone poster that lists goals, shows progress, and details incentives if goals are reached. Have separate rewards for yourself, such as a spa day or other important elements of self-care that motivate you. Use anything you can to inspire positive attitudes and change.

When considering the changes you will make, remember that the success of your bridge does not depend on how beautiful or high it is, or what others think of it. Rather, success is determined by you and what your family needs. The bridge must be functional, useful, and effective in helping raise your children and creating a strong, supportive family. In the beginning, you may need to focus primarily on the big stones, like structure and safety. Then, as you continue the process, you will be able to concentrate more on smaller rocks and mortar. These include implementing the tools you learned in this book, your values, unique family traditions, and way of building a life. Every small effort will come together to help strengthen your bridge and hold it all in place. The foundation you establish and the bridge you build will gradually lead you to a place of greater safety, optimism, and confidence.

ADDITIONAL RESOURCES

To build a stronger bridge for better behavior, explore the various resources and additional services available on our website at http://www.healthyfoundations.co. There you can sign up for our free newsletter, subscribe to The Parenting Bridge podcast, and link to our YouTube channel for lots of helpful videos. Finally, join us on social media at:

Facebook - www.facebook.com/HealthyFoundationsFamilyProgram
Instagram - www.instragram.com/healthyfoundationsfp/.

For direct parent support, we offer remote and in-person coaching with a variety of packages designed to help you build a stronger parenting foundation, problem-solve difficult situations, and find hope. We also offer the Healthy Foundations Family Program®, which includes a ninety-day intensive online program with one-on-one coaching, group support, and thirty days of videos for the first month. If you are struggling with high levels of destructive behaviors and aggression, I recommend our four-day, in-home intensive to provide a more solid family reset. Again, visit our website to learn more or reach out to discuss your situation with a member of our team.

Begin building a better bridge for your family today by following these steps:

1. Visit our website and enroll in our online parenting course
2. Schedule a call with our office to address your questions and discuss availability
3. Start connecting with us on our social media platforms

ACKNOWLEDGEMENTS

I want to thank my parents, Bill and Paula Jones, for their commitment to parenting. They started their family with me when I was six years old. Growing up, I might have questioned their parenting, and I sure had a lot of my own ideas on how it should be done. But, after raising half-a-dozen children and working with adoptive parents and kids for years, I know what they did was not easy. I had a hard start to life, and back then there was not a great deal of information about parenting children from hard places. They gave it their best despite the challenges and I always appreciated how intentional they were with me. I'm thankful also for the books on parenting, primarily Dr. Dobson, that I found and read. Thank you for giving me a family with so many opportunities. Thank you, Mom and Dad, for showing me about family in a way I would not have learned had you not adopted me.

Without the immense support of Kevin Mullani and Innovator Press pushing me along as I continued to work in the homes, teaching and training parents, developing our staff and the Healthy Foundation Family Program, this book would not have been completed. I am incredibly thankful to Kevin and Stephanie because from the first time we met, I felt they understood the need for this book.

There are others who have been incredibly supportive and encouraging such as Jo Wenger, my amazing office manager and chief of operations at Healthy Foundations. My husband, Merlin Flake, and his family. My colleague and friend, Dr. Ronald Federici, along with many other experts and their work in the field such as Dr. Dave Ziegler and Russell Barkley.

I also owe a debt of gratitude to my children who have served as some of my best teachers. I always wanted to be a mom and raise a big family. I made more than my fair share of mistakes along the way, but I learned and grew as a parent and a person because of my amazing family.

Lastly, a huge thanks to the families who have put their trust in our help at Healthy Foundations and allowed me and my team countless hours in their homes to guide them in such a precious and sensitive area as parenting.

END NOTES

CHAPTER 1

1. CDC.gov
2. Hurr & Wulcyzn, 2020 McKee et al., 2018; Pishva, 2017
3. Jones, 2017
4. Jones, 2017
5. Clossey et al., 2018; McPherson et al., 2018
6. Clossey et al., 2018; McPherson et al., 2018
7. Duncombe et al, 2016, Blocher-Rubin & Krabill, 2017, Clossey et al, 2018
8. Huhr & Wulczyn, 2020
9. Tully et al., 2017
10. Chen et al., 2016
11. Clossey et al, 2018
12. Clossey et al, 2018

CHAPTER 5

1. cyc-net.org
2. Van der Kolk, B (2005). Developmental trauma disorder: Towards a rational diagnosis for children with complex trauma histories Psychiatric Annuals, 33, 5. Pp 401-408

3. Van der Kolk, B (2005). Developmental trauma disorder: Towards a rational diagnosis for children with complex trauma histories Psychiatric Annuals, 33, 5. Pp 401-408

4. Perry,B. (2006) Applying principles of neurodevelopment to clinical work with maltreated and traumatized children. In N Webb (Ed.) Working with traumatized youth in child welfare (pp 27-52). New York: Guilford Press.

CHAPTER 7

1. Sokyahealthdev."Your Brain Thrives on Positivity." SokyaHealth, November 29, 2020, https://www.sokyahealth.com/mood/your-brain-thrives-on-positivity/

CHAPTER 8

1. Perry, Bruce D., and Oprah Winfrey. *What happened to you?: Conversations on trauma, resilience, and healing.* New York, New York: Flatiron, 2021.

CHAPTER 11

1. Bratton, William, and George Kelling. "Why We Need Broken Window Policing." City Journal, December 2014.

www.ingramcontent.com/pod-product-compliance
Lightning Source LLC
Chambersburg PA
CBHW040304170426
43194CB00021B/2887